PALEO LUNCHES
and Breakfasts
^ON THE GO

THE SOLUTION TO GLUTEN-FREE EATING ALL DAY LONG WITH DELICIOUS, EASY AND PORTABLE PRIMAL MEALS

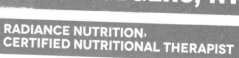

DIANA RODGERS, NTP

RADIANCE NUTRITION,
CERTIFIED NUTRITIONAL THERAPIST

PAGE STREET
PUBLISHING CO.

PAGE STREET
PUBLISHING CO.

First published in 2013 by
Page Street Publishing
27 Congress Street, Suite 103
Salem, MA 01970
www.pagestreetpublishing.com

Distributed by Macmillan; sales in Canada by The Canadian Manda Group; distribution in Canada by The Jaguar Book Group.

16 15 14 13   5

ISBN-13: 978-1-62414-016-7
ISBN-10: 1-62414-016-5

Library of Congress Control Number: 2013931986

Cover and book design by Page Street Publishing
Photography by Teri Lyn Fisher
Farm photography by Diana Rodgers and Frank Proctor

Printed and bound in China

Page Street is proud to be a member of 1% for the Planet. Members donate one percent of their sales to one or more of the over 1,500 environmental and sustainability charities across the globe who participate in this program.

To Anson and Phoebe, my amazing little
kids who will one day do great things

Contents

FOREWORD   6

INTRODUCTION   7

CHAPTER 1
Grab-and-Go Paleo Wraps   27

CHAPTER 2
Cook-and-Run Paleo Wraps   59

CHAPTER 3
Portable, Primal Salads   81

CHAPTER 4
Office-Ready Soups and Stews   102

CHAPTER 5
Busy Morning Breakfasts   118

CHAPTER 6
Entry-Level Essentials   147

CHAPTER 7
Snappy Sides   158

CHAPTER 8
Day-to-Day Dressings   177

RESOURCES   185

ACKNOWLEDGEMENTS   188

ABOUT THE AUTHOR   189

INDEX   190

Foreword

HI THERE! I'M ROBB WOLF, *New York Times* bestselling author of *The Paleo Solution*, Dad to Zoe, husband to Nicki and a former research biochemist in the areas of cancer and autoimmunity. I am also a friend of Diana Rodgers and a huge fan of her work. She has a deep understanding of Paleo nutrition that is unrivaled and this cookbook is exactly what the Paleo community needs.

As a former research biochemist, most of my education was pretty tough: covering everything from physics and calculus to quantum mechanics and LOTS of chemistry. But I've got to say, the past 13 years of talking to people about Paleo nutrition has presented one consistent theme that makes my academic coursework seem pretty easy by comparison and that is helping people to feed themselves in a way that is healthy, time-effective and fun.

I'm pretty handy in the kitchen so I always assumed other folks were as well. This is like assuming that because I can run a gas-chromatograph/mass-spectrometer that I can fix a car! But I actually receive the most gnashing of teeth when folks are trying to figure out breakfast and lunch, especially if they are eating out or on the road. And that is why this book is so important; many people are a bit hamstrung when it comes to getting the day started with a tasty, healthy breakfast or packing a solid lunch, let alone keeping it Paleo.

We're in luck! Diana Rodgers has taken her knowledge of Paleo nutrition, sprinkled in advice on how to navigate the kitchen and feed a family, simmered on low and produced this fantastic work, *Paleo Lunches and Breakfasts on the Go*. This book covers everything you will need to make delicious, time-efficient Paleo meals. You will see meals inspired by a number of different ethnic cuisines while also getting acquainted with sustainability.

With this book, you'll become a locavore that even Michael Pollan would be proud of.

Introduction

In my work as a nutritional therapist and consultant, I meet a lot of Paleo dieters. Most of them love the benefits of their diet but struggle with the practicalities of maintaining it all day long. Breakfast and lunch are where most people get stuck. It can be challenging to grab a quick and satisfying Paleo lunch while on a short break from work. Leftovers from home eventually feel boring and uninspired—there's only so much leftover chili you can take to work! This book is designed just for you: the busy Paleo dieter. Whether you're plugging away at a sixty-hour-a-week office job or managing kids and a household with little time to plan meals, you need lunch and breakfast options that are easy, delicious and portable.

I know the meaning of busy. My typical day includes running my own business; darting from my workouts to graduate school classes; seeing nutrition clients and picking up my kids at school. I've got a fast-action life and it has inspired me to create some easy solutions for tasty lunches and breakfasts that are Paleo compliant. I've also paid my dues in the corporate world and understand what it's like to be rushing out the door in the morning when it's still dark out and not have time to plan something enticing for lunch—never mind squeezing in a healthy breakfast. Do you feel like everyone but you has a great choice for lunch? Just wait until you see all the delicious and quick-to-assemble dishes that will soon liven up your workday and reinvigorate your diet. In the Grab-and-Go Paleo Wraps chapter, you'll find easy-to-make lettuce wraps like the Turkey Apricot Dijon Wrap and the Roast Beef and Celeriac Slaw Wrap. Tasty wraps like these take mere minutes to make but are so incredibly delicious to eat. You'll be surprised by the number of speedy, gourmet breakfasts—like the Cherry Tarragon Breakfast Sausages—that can be assembled in minutes with commonly found ingredients. No culinary degree necessary! From soups to wraps to mouth-watering salads, the recipes in this book are your answer to eating a healthy Paleo diet on the go.

MY PATH TO PALEO

As a young child, I struggled to gain weight and was often sick. I was hospitalized for dehydration several times and suffered from severe nosebleeds, low muscle tone and an overall lack of energy. I was always hungry and in digestive distress. My doctor thought my symptoms were caused by lactose intolerance and recommended that I continue to drink soy milk (I was fed soy formula from day one) instead of cow's milk. It didn't help.

After college, I stopped drinking soda and eating junk food. I thought I was doing everything right by eating a low-fat, whole grain and mostly vegetarian diet. When I was diagnosed with celiac disease in my mid-twenties and had to give up wheat, I felt like I had the most restrictive diet anyone could possibly follow. I had been eating wheat three times a day, so just making the switch to gluten-free food was an enormous adjustment. After attending a Weston A. Price conference in my early thirties, I started to eat butter and other good fats. I felt much better, but it wasn't until I did the 30-day Paleo challenge, as prescribed in *The Paleo Solution*, that I really felt "cured." For me, eating healthy has been a lifelong journey.

No matter how hard you have struggled with your health, the important thing is to keep trying. If you haven't already done so, get a good book on Paleo, check out some recipes and practice making nutrient-dense meals like the ones that follow.

THE RULES

The Paleo Diet (Paleo being short for Paleolithic Era) is based on eating the most nutrient-dense foods that cause the least amount of irritation to the body. This includes meats, vegetables and fruit. The Paleo diet requires the elimination of all refined sugars, grains, legumes and dairy products that are so common in the Standard American Diet. Most people who start this diet begin with a 30-day Paleo challenge where they are 100 percent compliant, then move into a blend of about 80/20, where 80 percent of their diet is Paleo and 20 percent is not. Some foods like dairy and a number of starches are heavily debated in the Paleo community. Regardless of where you stand on these foods, stay focused on the primary goal of eating nutrient-dense foods to achieve optimal health.

Here are some basic Paleo rules:

• Cut out wheat, sugar, all grains, legumes and dairy.*

• Cut down on coffee—no more than 1 cup (235 ml) per day.

• Change all the fats in your house to healthy ones.

• Invest in a C.S.A. or grow your own veggies.

• Find a good source for pasture-raised meat and eggs.

• Start moving your body on a regular basis: Lift weights, sprint and have fun.

*See my note on dairy later in this chapter (page 15). After their 30-day introduction to the Paleo diet, some people do very well with certain types of dairy.

THE PAYOFF

The payoff to maintaining your Paleo diet is huge. According to the *European Journal of Clinical Nutrition*, "Even short-term (10-day) consumption of a Paleolithic type diet improves blood pressure and glucose tolerance, decreases insulin secretion, increases insulin sensitiv-ity and improves lipid profiles." When you eat Paleo, you have more energy to play with your kids, engage in a sport you love or simply go for a nice walk with a friend after work. There is no mid-morning blood sugar crash or afternoon drowsiness, both of which are common among adults who start their day with cereal and follow it up with a sandwich, a soda and a bag of chips for lunch. Eventually your clothes will fit better, your workouts will improve and you will enjoy a faster recovery thanks to decreased inflammation. Your body will have more efficient hormonal responses, which will lower your stress and improve your personal life (if you know what I mean). Thanks to this diet, you will enjoy a stronger immune system and will be less likely to develop a chronic disease. If your doctor is concerned about your lipid profile, those numbers will most likely improve on the Paleo diet.

You deserve to enjoy (or continue to enjoy) all the fantastic benefits of eating Paleo no matter how busy you are. This book is your ticket to a low-maintenance, everyday Paleo diet. With mouthwatering recipes that are simple to follow, anyone can be a pro! Give it a try and I guarantee you'll love the results.

HOW TO START YOUR PALEO JOURNEY

Maybe you bought this book because you're already eating a Paleo diet and need some creative ideas for breakfast and lunch; maybe you've just started the plan and you're struggling; perhaps you're trying to convert a loved one or friend to Paleo. If you are new to the diet, I've found there are two basic ways to transition to eating Paleo. One way is "cold turkey" and the other I call "baby steps." Depending on your own personal situation, one might be more effective than the other. There is no right answer for everyone.

Cold Turkey: This approach works great for those with serious issues affecting their health or who already eat pretty well and need to just take that next step and do a 30-day Paleo challenge.

Baby Steps: This begins with cutting out wheat and sugar, which is a *huge* step that can result in amazing changes. I usually suggest remaining at this stage for about one month while continuing to eat dairy and gluten-free foods. After a month, breakfast transitions to Paleo for the first two weeks, then both breakfast and lunch become Paleo compliant for the third and fourth weeks. Finally, start your 30-day challenge of squeaky-clean 100 percent Paleo: no grains, legumes, dairy or sweeteners. There is nothing wrong with taking the "baby steps" path. For some of my clients, this is a much easier way to transition to a lifestyle that may be dramatically different from their previous one.

HOW I STARTED

Mine was more of a "baby steps" journey. I had already been gluten free for several years when I took the 30-day Paleo challenge I read about in *The Paleo Solution*. The book made so much sense to me that I immediately eliminated almost all starch from my diet and focused on meat and vegetables. At first, I was extremely tired. For about two to three weeks, I felt like I was on Benadryl all day long. After that time however, I experienced a sense of boundless energy. I couldn't believe the results! I went from experiencing incredible, splitting headaches almost every day, having the urge to eat every two hours, and getting shaky and disoriented if I were to skip a meal to a feeling of absolute calm. I was able to make it from breakfast to lunch without a snack! The period between lunch and dinner also became snack free since I was no longer ravenous at 4 p.m.

I used to wake up with a vision of what I'd cook for dinner and then spend the entire day dreaming about when I'd get to eat the (insert highly glycemic food here). On the Paleo diet, my food cravings vanished. I was finally liberated from my food addictions and the feeling was incredible. I no longer needed to carry a bag full of gluten-free bars, nuts and fruit with me at all times. My digestion improved. I lost that layer of post-baby weight and returned to the size I was in

high school. After my 30-day challenge, I slowly reintroduced Paleo-friendly starches, turned in my spinning instructor card and joined a CrossFit gym.

With the help of the Paleo diet, I've never felt stronger and healthier in my entire life. I've played around a bit with my macronutrient balance and I feel like I have a good sense of how my body wants to me to be eating. When, in the past, I dipped into super-low carb territory (like under 50 g/2 oz a day) it made me very unhappy and, well, let's just say unpleasant to be around. I now know that being super-low carb just doesn't work for me. I generally keep my carbs around 75–125 g/3-5 oz per day, depending on my workout schedule. I don't weigh my food or count my calories. I find I do best with no starch at breakfast but a little starch at lunch and dinner. My husband and my trainer can both attest to the fact that when I refuel with some good starch, I'm a much nicer person and preform better in the gym.

What I learned: Adjust your portions and carbohydrates to fit your size and lifestyle. Basically, what's good for me is not necessarily what's good for you. Use your own body to figure out what portions and foods make you feel your best. I strongly dislike the one-size-fits-all diets and BMI markers for health. In my twenties I may have weighed less, but my body fat percentage is much lower today! My digestion is 100 percent better and I'm healthier and stronger, so who cares if I'm a lot heavier from all of the muscle I've gained lifting weights? If we only use a scale to judge our overall health, we are missing the bigger picture.

What's an appropriate food and portion size for an active, fit, twenty-five-year-old male is not the same for a sedentary seventy-five-year-old woman recovering from hip replacement surgery. In short, follow the basic Paleo template and adjust as needed for your specific situation. Are you very active? You may need to increase your starchy carbohydrate intake to see better performance in the gym. Are you overweight and metabolically deranged? A relatively lower carbohydrate diet is most likely the best place to start.

It's always important to consider your goals when on the Paleo diet. Common goals for my clients are fat loss, healing or better performance in the gym. These three goals reflect very different macronutrient ratios. What's a good Paleo diet for one client may not be ideal for another.

LET'S TALK FOOD: WHAT'S PALEO FRIENDLY?

HYDRATION SOURCES

For drinking, try water, sparkling water, herbal teas and coffee substitutes. I actually like the taste of a coffee substitute such as Teechino which you can find at most large natural grocery stores. Too much water with your meal can dilute your stomach acid and enzymes and mess with digestion. Drink two glasses of water a half hour before eating and wait two hours after eating to drink more. Avoid alcohol but if you must, tequila, gin or vodka mixed with soda water and a little lime or lemon is the best choice because it's easiest on your liver. However, on your 30-Day Paleo challenge, you should eliminate alcohol.

FAT SOURCES

For cooking, use coconut oil, butter, ghee, bacon fat, tallow and lard. Olive oil is great for salads and low-heat cooking but I prefer more saturated fats for high-heat cooking. Foods that are good sources of fat include avocados, egg yolks (from pastured chickens) and fatty cuts of meat from pastured animals.

PROTEIN SOURCES

Eggs, fish, shellfish, beef, pork, lamb (ideally grass-fed or wild), chicken and turkey are good sources of protein. Game meats like venison, elk and other herbivores are excellent. Meat from grass-fed animals is ideal for many ethical and environmental reasons. It is also

Know Your Egg Terms

There are lots of different ways to raise chickens and some of the terms can be confusing to the public. Here are the differences between them:

"Eggs" The typical eggs sold in most grocery stores come from chickens raised in cramped cages and usually given antibiotics. Artificial lights are often used to increase egg productivity. Conditions are stressful and cramped, and the air in these facilities is thick with dust and ammonia. This technique is banned in some areas of Europe.

"Cage Free" This term doesn't really mean much. These chickens simply were not in small cages but are typically raised indoors in crowded conditions. In addition, there is no guarantee the chickens weren't given antibiotics or fed anything other than grain.

"Fed Vegetarian Feed, All-Natural, Farm-Fresh, Omega-3 Eggs" This just means the chickens were fed grain and possibly other vegetable matter but they did not get access to the outside (or else they would have consumed bugs and even mice, which is what chickens *love* to eat). In fact, these words mean nothing as far as the welfare of the chickens is concerned and, most of the time, they are raised in cages. Omega-3 eggs might have more omega-3 from some additional flax seeds in their grain mix, but don't think these birds got to see the light of the outdoors.

"Humane" and "Certified Organic" If you don't have access to farmer-raised or backyard chicken eggs and a supermarket is your only option, look for eggs that are labeled "humane" and "certified organic" (meaning they consumed organic grain).

ideal from a health perspective as it contains more anti-inflammatory long-chain omega-3 fatty acids. Organ meats, such as liver, are very rich sources of vitamins and can be included in your diet on a weekly basis. Sausage and bacon are great but be careful—sometimes breadcrumbs or other gluten-containing ingredients are added to sausages. Another common ingredient in sausages and other processed food is "hydrolyzed vegetable protein" which may contain gluten.

Choosing Eggs:

All of my egg dishes call for eggs from pasture-raised chickens. There are several reasons for this. Most notably, they are a significantly better source of long-chain omega-3 fatty acids than eggs from chickens that have eaten grain exclusively. The "organic" label on eggs usually means the chicken has been fed organic grain, but not necessarily their natural diet of grass and bugs, which is what pastured chickens consume. On my farm, we raise our chickens in mobile coops, rotating them around the farm to fresh pasture on a regular basis. Their constant scratching at the ground and droppings fertilize the soil. They get fresh grass and bugs to eat, lots of sunlight and fresh air, are healthier and stronger than conventionally raised chickens and are subjected to much less stress than birds who are raised in C.A.F.O.s (Concentrated Animal Feeding Operations).

FRUIT

If you're looking to lose weight, moderating your fruit intake is a good idea. Berries and citrus fruits are your best choices. Lemons and limes can help the liver break down fats, and they are relatively low in fructose. They also add nice flavoring to your water!

VEGETABLES

The benefits of vegetables come from their vitamin and antioxidant content. Vegetables are great at making you feel full while you're consuming fewer calories. This is useful if you're looking to lose weight. Some vegetables are okay to eat raw, like lettuce and other easily digestible greens. However, I prefer most of my vegetables cooked. In particular, cruciferous vegetables like kale, cabbage, bok choy and broccoli should always be cooked in order to lower the goitrogen content and break down cell walls for better nutrient absorption. Spinach, Swiss chard and beets should also be cooked to reduce their oxalic acid content.

STARCHES

It's best to consume the bulk of your daily starch intake in a post-workout meal. I know most people who write about the Paleo diet are against eating white potatoes. In my opinion, *peeled* white potatoes are an excellent source of starch to replenish glycogen stores after working out. White potatoes are higher in calories than sweet potatoes and winter squash, but as far as digestion goes, most people without an active autoimmune disease do very well with white potatoes. I personally prefer the taste to sweet potatoes but either one can be used in these recipes. If eating potatoes freaks you out, try roots like yucca and batata, which can be found in Latin markets.

SALT

Natural sea salt has the best profile of minerals. Keep in mind that you'll be missing out on the iodine added to conventional salt, so be sure to get some iodine from seaweed once a week or so.

SWEETENERS

Try to avoid sweeteners. If you must have a sweetener, pure dextrose, Stevia, honey and maple syrup are okay for a special treat once in while. Enjoy them sparingly after your 30-day challenge.

CONDIMENTS, HERBS AND SPICES

In trying to cut out sugar, it may be helpful to naturally sweeten a meal by using spices that have sweet flavors like allspice, anise, cinnamon, cloves, ginger and nutmeg. I also frequently use cumin, coriander, cardamom, thyme, fresh ginger, basil and paprika. Dijon mustard, vinegars (avoid malt vinegar), coconut aminos (found at natural food stores like Whole Foods or online) and tomato paste are great staples for your cabinet.

NUTS

I've included a few recipes that include nuts, but in general I don't eat a ton of nuts. Nuts are very calorically dense and easy to eat in excess, especially when salted. Also, the proper way to prepare nuts is to soak raw nuts and dehydrate before eating, which few people have the time to do. Tip: If you have an active autoimmune disease, nuts should be avoided.

FLOURS

I know there are a lot of Paleo cookbooks out there with baked goods recipes that call for nut flours. I'm not a big fan of Paleo treats made with nut flours. I also don't believe people should be eating sweet muffins, cookies and other baked goods on a regular basis. When I do make baked goods, I use flours that contain less polyunsaturated fat to minimize the amount of toxic compounds formed during the baking process. Coconut flour, tapioca starch and potato starch are my go-to flours for Paleo baked goods.

PALEO GUIDE TO DINING OUT

I know you're busy. Maybe you travel a lot or have a crazy work schedule. There may be days when you don't have time to pack a lunch. That's the whole reason for this book—to help you stay committed to eating Paleo even when your life is hectic. Here are a few tips to use when you don't have a lunch from home or when you want to dine out with friends or coworkers. Many restaurants can be made Paleo friendly except for big-chain pasta places. When in doubt, opt for a small mom-and-pop restaurant where they make all of their food in house or a high-end restaurant where items are more often made to order. It's always best to find a place where there is actually a chef back there in the kitchen.

Tip: Just because something is Paleo doesn't mean it's good for you to consume in large quantities. You will not lose weight eating an extra-large bag of almonds every day or by chasing every meal with a pint of coconut milk. Be sensible. You shouldn't be hungry, but you shouldn't eat to full capacity either.

Tip: When you're at a restaurant, it's crucial to communicate what you can and can't have. Over the years, I've learned to use the word "flour" instead of saying "wheat" which gets confused for "meat", and I avoid saying "gluten" which can sometimes bring a blank stare from the server. I've found that keeping my request specific and menu choices simple is the best tactic to getting what I want.

Paleo Guide to Dining Out

Mexican

Choose a salad with meat, guacamole and fresh salsa (no cheese, beans or rice). Another option is fajitas without tortillas and with extra veggies. Be careful of marinades and seasonings for the meat; I've seen wheat-based soy sauce added to fajitas before. Avoid soups that could be made from bouillon cubes or canned broth with gluten added.

Indian

Tandoori chicken, meat and vegetable curry dishes are safe. Be sure to ask what they use to thicken their sauces. It could be flour. If you're sensitive to dairy, many of their sauces are thickened with cream or yogurt instead of coconut milk, so double check that, too!

Brazilian BBQ

This is one of my favorites! Most Brazilian food is gluten free. The meats are delicious and the stews are usually thickened with tapioca starch (also called cassava or yucca root).

American

If I'm at a standard American restaurant or pub, my go-to meal is a salad with steak tips, salmon or chicken breast, and avocado. Ask if you can have your meat plain, meaning without the marinade. Try a side salad with an order of your favorite dish minus the rice/french fries/pasta. Avoid barbecue sauces as they can have tons of sugar. A burger with no bun and a side salad is also a good choice. Lemon and olive oil make a Paleo-friendly dressing. Don't forget to specify no croutons on your salad.

Vietnamese

Vietnamese is my go-to lunch when I'm feeling run down. I get a noodle soup bowl with double meat, extra steamed vegetables and no noodles. Most authentic Vietnamese restaurants make their broth in house and do not tend to add soy sauce or other gluten products to their broth.

Japanese

Gluten can sneak into sushi through spicy mayo sauce which can have soy sauce in it. Beware of "crunchy," meaning deep-fried, items with panko bread crumbs in sushi rolls. Fancy rolls can sometimes also be drizzled in a sauce that might not be listed on the menu. That seaweed salad you love and think is so healthy is usually made with all kinds of chemical dyes, preservatives and corn syrup. Your best bet is to stick with plain sashimi and bring your own gluten-free soy sauce or coconut aminos.

Chinese

This is a cuisine I pretty much avoid unless I know the owners and they really understand everything I can't eat and are willing to make me something off the menu. There's just so much to worry about at a Chinese restaurant since gluten and MSG are pretty much standard in every item.

Italian

It is actually pretty easy to get a good Paleo meal at high-end Italian restaurants. It's the large chain Italian places, or the small pizza- and pasta-only restaurants that I avoid. Italian menus can really vary depending on the restaurant, but you can usually find some delicious

(continued on next page)

marinated olives, mushrooms and other vegetables for an appetizer. When it comes to your entree, skip the pasta and head straight for the meat. Make sure there is no flour used to coat the meat before it's cooked. Have a side of vegetables, being sure to ask if they're blanched in the pasta water (yeah, really!). I'll usually have a big salad and a nice, slow-roasted osso bucco or a piece of fish when I am out at an Italian restaurant.

Breakfast

Special attention should be paid when eating out for breakfast. I don't really go out for breakfast because gluten sneaks into so many morning dishes. Some large chain restaurants will even mix a little pancake batter into the eggs when making omelets to make them fluffier. You know that egg mix stuff they use in hotels and cafeterias? It's made with eggs, nonfat dry milk, soybean oil and salt. See if your favorite breakfast restaurant will make you fried eggs in a separate pan (not on the griddle where the pancakes and French toast were fried) with a side of sautéed vegetables and maybe a small steak. I've gotten sick so many times after eating out for breakfast that I now only do so when I have no other options.

If you're like me, once you start eating Paleo, you'll soon find that unless it's a really great restaurant, or you're in a time pinch, it's just not worth the money to go out to a mediocre meal when you can cook such amazing food right in your own home for much less.

Paleo for Busy Travelers

Here are some tips for your next vacation or work trip:

1. Try to book a room with a kitchen. Better yet, my family likes to stay in apartments. We not only get a kitchen where we can cook delicious Paleo meals, but we also enjoy some extra space and get a much better night's sleep.

2. Find out where the local farmers markets are located, and load up on fresh eggs, meats and vegetables. I really love visiting markets in other cities to see what the farmers are growing and to check out how they display their produce.

3. If you travel by car, consider bringing some Paleo basics with you. We bring pastured eggs and bacon with us, as I know they will be superior to anything we find on the road. Snacks for the car are usually a little fruit and some homemade jerky.

4. If you're flying, pack cured meat like salami and hard-boiled eggs in your carry-on bag. If you're stuck in a standard hotel room, bring a few cans of sardines or tuna and skip the standard continental breakfast in the lobby. There's no sense in eating the free breakfast if you have to pay for it later.

COMMON QUESTIONS

CAN I CHEAT A LITTLE?

Some people can get away with more cheating and others have to be stricter. Most people start off their introduction to the Paleo diet with a 30-day strict phase then transition to an 80/20 rule (80 percent of the time they eat strict Paleo and 20 percent of the time they don't). Those with health conditions usually need to stick to more of a 95 percent compliance to the Paleo diet. A word of caution though—I've seen the 80/20 rule get pretty out of hand very quickly. It's good to check in with yourself weekly and honestly assess how much you are cheating.

After your 30-day strict phase, if you're going to have a cheat, try to keep it gluten free, write the food down in your food journal (if you keep one, which you should if you're trying to lose weight) and closely monitor how you look and feel for the next week or so. When I have a cheat, it's usually the following items: an occasional corn tortilla, a little rice, some gluten-free bread, a small bowl of really great ice cream or some dark chocolate.

Planning an epic cheat for a Friday night where you can binge on pizza, pasta, beer and ice cream is another story. I'm opposed to planned cheat days as they are really counterproductive to what you've accomplished all week. Besides, some of the foods you'll be having on cheat day are addictive. Bingeing on these foods is playing with fire and becomes something similar to an eating disorder. Try to remember how much you enjoy the way your pants fit, and how great you feel while eating clean. If you must cheat, the safest choice is to make the cheats small, infrequent and gluten free.

SOME OF YOUR RECIPES INCLUDE DAIRY. WHAT'S UP WITH THAT?

I do have a few recipes in the book, like the Superhero Chicken Liver Pâté (page 163), that call for the optional addition of cream, butter or *fermented* dairy. Ideally, you should omit all dairy food for your 30-day Paleo challenge. If you would like to reintroduce it after that period, record how you feel as you do so. Dairy can cause acne or stuffiness in some people and digestive issues in others. Casein, a protein in milk, can also be problematic in some people. I happen to feel fine with a little raw and fermented dairy in my diet. Plain whole milk yogurts, crème fraîche and raw milk cheeses are a great source C.L.A. (conjugated linoleic acid) and fat-soluble vitamins. So unless it gives you a problem, certain forms of dairy can be a great nutrient-dense addition to your diet. Consider the benefits of including small amounts of good dairy items in your diet. Processed dairy foods with poor nutrient density on the other hand—like low-fat, ultra-pasteurized chocolate milk, American cheese and low-fat, fruit-flavored yogurts which are high in sugar should be avoided altogether.

WHAT ABOUT ALL THE SODIUM AND THOSE NITRATES IN DELI MEATS AND BACON: ARE YOU TRYING TO KILL ME?

Unless you have a medical issue restricting sodium, the sodium in deli meats is no big deal in the context of a healthy Paleo diet. I actually see more people with *too little* salt in their diet on Paleo than too much. Basically, I don't sweat a few nitrates on occasion. I think bacon and other cured meats, especially from pastured pigs like those I raise on my farm, are an excellent, nutrient dense food. In 2012, Chris Kresser wrote a great piece on his website called "The Nitrate and Nitrite Myth: Another Reason not to Fear Bacon." Here is a short excerpt from the article on ChrisKresser.com:

"The study that originally connected nitrates with cancer risk and caused the scare in the first place has since been discredited after being subjected to a peer review. There have been major reviews of the scientific literature that found no link between nitrates or nitrites and human cancers, or even evidence to suggest that they may be carcinogenic. Further, recent research suggests that nitrates and nitrites may not only be harmless, they may be beneficial, especially for immunity and heart health."

WHAT ABOUT YOUR SUGGESTIONS TO WARM UP FOOD IN THE MICROWAVE? NOW I KNOW YOU'RE TRYING TO KILL ME!

Microwave use is absolutely fine for reheating as long as the food container is not plastic. I use glass containers for any meal that I am reheating in a microwave. I even have a recipe for poaching an egg in a glass of water in a microwave and it comes out perfectly! Microwaves do denature proteins, but so does regular cooking. From a scientific standpoint, the chemical structure of food is not altered from a microwave any more than from regular cooking. Please don't be scared off from using a microwave to occasionally reheat your leftovers.

THE AUTOIMMUNE PALEO PROTOCOL

If you have an active autoimmune disease, there are a few extra foods that most Paleo experts suggest you pull from your diet, at least temporarily to see how you feel. In addition to refined sugar, dairy, all grains and legumes, it is suggested that those with an active autoimmune condition also temporarily remove nuts and seeds, eggs and nightshades. Tomatoes, eggplants, white potatoes and peppers (including the spices made from peppers like cayenne and paprika) are all part of the nightshade family. If there still seem to be some major digestive issues, you can also consider removing the group of foods classified as "F.O.D.M.A.P.s"

(Fermentable Oligosaccharides, Disaccharides, Monosaccharides And Polyols). You can do a simple internet search to find out if you're currently consuming high F.O.D.M.A.P. foods that could be contributing to your digestive issues. There are a few gut-healing protocols available today, such as the G.A.P.S. Diet, but these reintroduce dairy too early in my opinion. Sticking with no dairy until all digestive issues are under control would be best. Diane Sanfilippo's book, *Practical Paleo: A Customized Approach to Health and a Whole-Foods Lifestyle* has an excellent guide to cooking with the autoimmune Paleo protocol in mind.

MAKING PALEO WORK WITH KIDS

As a mother of two active kids, I can say that, in general, kids are more open-minded about food than most people give them credit for. If you keep offering good choices and eliminate bad choices from your house, your kids will adjust to eating better. The cold turkey v. baby steps scenario also works with kids. If you want to go cold turkey, simply eliminate all non-Paleo choices from your house. Depending on your kid's personality, he'll generally put up a fight for a few days and then adjust pretty quickly. I used a sneakier, more gradual approach. I'd say, "The store was out of orange juice today." I switched their bread to gluten-free bread, started packing more protein and fruit in their lunch boxes instead of crackers and granola bars and slowly replaced classic snack foods with healthier options. Today, Paleo-friendly options are a norm for them.

TIPS FOR THE PALEO PARENT:

You're the Boss.

You don't let them choose between doing homework and watching TV, right? They *have to* do their home-work. Well it's the same with good food. You are the one making the choices about what comes into the house (assuming they're not old enough to drive to the store and buy their own food). Make good choices for meals and that's that.

Keep carbohydrates in their diet.

Kids have limited glycogen storage capacity due to their size but many can expend more calories than an adult. Assuming they are active and healthy, kids need a higher carbohydrate ratio than adults.

Avoid bonding over bonbons.

In my practice, many of the moms I see have a really hard time giving this one up. They associate baking sugary treats with bonding with their kids. Creating this reward pathway doesn't help children become adults with healthy attitudes toward food. There are other ways of bonding with kids than baking cupcakes. Going out into nature or making another non-food-related craft at home is just as much fun, and you won't have a plate full of sugar staring you in the face at the end.

Teach the benefits of food.

When our kids were very little, changing their food was easy. Now that they're a little older, my husband and I focus on the nutrient content of certain foods. Carrots can give you "super night vision," for example. When our son was in his Star Wars phase, we told him that his dinner was full of Midi-chlorians, the special Jedi life force. We also use athletic performance as an incentive: I'd say, "The meat in this stew will build strong muscles for hitting that baseball and the sweet potatoes will help you run really fast to the base."

Prep for birthday parties and playdates.

When kids are little, you can pack healthy snacks for them and avoid playdates at mealtime so that they eat how you want them to. Now that my kids are a bit older, I try to send them to playdates and parties with a full belly and a healthy attitude. That way, when they do eat cake or other junk, they're likely to eat less of it. This also helps them to feel normal among their peers. I do my best to feed them optimal food when they're at home or at a restaurant with me, but when they're

on their own I want them to feel empowered to make good choices. Other than some rowdy behavior from the sugar, I haven't noticed any adverse side effects (like poor indigestion). They are aware that cookies and cake make them feel lousy, so I just point that out to them if they complain and remind them to make better choices in the future.

Get buy-in.

As your kids grow a bit older, it's a good idea to have them help in making their school lunch choices. I say this only because one day I packed my eight-year-old son a can of sardines (something he loves to eat at home) for lunch. He came home crying and said the kids were making fun of him for having such a stinky and strange lunch. The last thing I want is for him to feel insecure because of our family's food choices. We now have open discussions about their lunch choices and decide together which healthy (and socially acceptable) foods I can pack. I'm sure I'll face more obstacles as my children grow older, but for now we're happily in agreement about lunch choices that satisfy us all. I've since discovered that the kids at my son's school think bacon and my Terrific Teriyaki Jerky (page 151) are super cool snacks to bring to school. All the other kids want a bite. Cool containers like the colorful divided LunchBots also make lunchtime more fun. Paleo can be popular!

Do your best.

Sometimes the transition to Paleo can take a while for kids. The simple act of going gluten free is a huge step in the right direction. If your kid strongly feels a sandwich is the only appropriate lunch food, choose some gluten-free bread with lots of good meat. Meat rollups are even better. Lunch can evolve into being more Paleo over time. Keep working at it and I'm sure you'll find certain Paleo foods that you can all agree upon. Pack them some protein, a little fruit and a bottle of water (there is no need for fruit juices at all for kids) and be happy your kids are eating well.

THREE WEEKS OF PALEO SCHOOL LUNCHES

(With bottled water for a drink)

	WEEK 1	WEEK 2	WEEK 3
MONDAY	Ham and pineapple cubes on skewers, handful of macadamia nuts	Hard-boiled eggs, carrot and pepper sticks, "Cheesy" Kale Chips (page 168), handful of grapes	Sliced Pork Teriyaki (from the Vietnamese "Bun" salad, page 85), all-natural apple-sauce, handful of hazelnuts
TUESDAY	Crisp Veggie and Turkey Rollup (page 38), strawberries on the side	Chicken, Vegetable and Avocado Soup (page 109, skip the avocado) with a side of Sea-Salted Rosemary Chive Crackers (page 175)	Bacon and Egg Salad (page 167, skip the onion and fresh herbs in my recipe) in a cup, a couple of slices of bacon, Sea-Salted Rosemary Chive Crackers (page 175), handful of cherry tomatoes
WEDNESDAY	Blueberry Cinnamon Coconut Smoothie (page 146), Terrific Teriyaki Jerky (page 151)	Bacon, Lemon and Greens Egg Muffins (page 138) made with all-natural hot dogs inside, cantaloupe slices	Terrific Teriyaki Jerky (page 151), dried apples and blueberries, cashews, fresh blood orange slices
THURSDAY	Sweet Apple Spice Breakfast Sausage (page 132) and Sweet Potato Apple-Cinnamon Pancakes (page 127)	Smoked Ham and Melon Wrap (page 35, skip the truffle oil) with carrot sticks and cherry tomatoes	Green salad with roasted chicken and Happy Valley Ranch Salad Dressing (page 181), Coconut Crepe (page 137) to wrap it in, fresh pear
FRIDAY	Mexican Chorizo Tacos (page 76, make the sausage mild), blackberries in a cup	Roasted chicken and pesto in a Sundried Tomato Rosemary Biscuit (page 154), fresh strawberries	Chicken or beef on skewers with Creamy Cashew Gado Gado Sauce (page 178), handful of fresh cherries

COMMON PALEO PITFALLS

Are you struggling with the Paleo diet? Are you overwhelmed with sugar cravings? Maybe the weight just isn't coming off. Here are some common mistakes I see in my practice that are holding people back from success:

1. Trying to Find Substitutes for Old Favorites. When you see new vegetarians, they are usually interested in meat substitutes for everything they are giving up. They reach for tofu hot dogs, meatless sausages and all kinds of processed foods. I did the same thing when I first went gluten free in my twenties. Breakfast was gluten-free toast, lunch was a gluten-free sandwich, and dinner was gluten-free pasta followed by a gluten free cookie, maybe with gluten-free beer. I see the same pattern in those new to the Paleo diet. They are trying to "Paleoize" all of their former foods. They miss bagels, muffins and cookies and are desperate to find substitutes. They are missing the big picture. While it's okay to have a Paleo muffin or cookie occasionally, the focus should be on real, nutrient-dense foods as opposed to mimicking the Standard American Diet with Paleo foods.

2. Limiting Fat. Fat is very satiating, slows absorption and is essential for absorption of certain nutrients. One of the biggest mistakes I see is people trying to do a Paleo diet on boneless, skinless chicken breast and steamed broccoli. Get yourself some grass-fed or pastured beef and eat the fat. Yes, fat makes things taste good, and it's also the "log" on the fire that will keep you running throughout the day.

3. Carb-Phobia. There's low-carb and then there's super-low carb. Anything under 50 g/2 oz of carbohydrates per day is super-low carb and can be pretty stressful on the system. There are some folks who need to eat this way for health reasons. However, if you're at all active and trying to do an intense cardio workout on zero carbs, you're just going to crash and burn. Carbs also reduce cortisol, so having some starch at night can help you sleep better.

4. Eating Too Little. This is another classic scenario that I often see, especially with women. They eat so little for lunch that by 4 p.m. they are seeing red. They reach for anything they can find. Don't let this be you: Make sure you are feeding yourself enough nutrient-dense foods throughout the day and have some snacks around in case you get extra hungry. If you are so hungry that you are making bad choices, then you are not eating enough or you are not eating the right things. Make sure each meal contains enough protein, fats and carbs in right ratio to fuel your endeavors.

5. Working Out Too Much. Over-training leads to higher cortisol levels, which can lead to weight gain. This is especially true for athletes addicted to cardio or highly glycogen-dependent sports. Try lifting a few times a week and doing some sprint work or rowing drills instead of running twenty miles five times a week.

6. Poor Sleep. Sleep is critical for healing and weight loss. Get eight hours of high-quality, uninterrupted sleep. Make sure you are in a completely dark room. Lack of sleep causes stress on the body and a stressed-out body will cling to weight, especially around the midsection. A stressed-out mind will seek out junk food, like sweets.

7. Going Nuts. *Nuts are Paleo, right? So why can't I eat them for snacks?* The answer to this common question is: You can have some nuts sometimes. I commonly see people complaining about not losing weight and when I look at their food journal, they are consuming a 5-pound (2,270 g) bag of almonds every day. Nuts won't really help you lose weight. If you're choosing between a cupcake and a handful of nuts, please go for the nuts. If you want to eat nuts and lose weight, keep the portions small (less than ten nuts per snack).

8. Epic Binging. Here's another one: *I only eat bad once a week or so.* When I look at the food journal of clients who say this, I see that it's an epic cheat meal full of beer, pizza, chips, etc. It's fine to have an occasional cheat meal, but these planned epic cheats of everything possible at one sitting are unhealthy. Have a bite of ice cream here and there, try to keep your cheats gluten free—and try to avoid binging on the entire kitchen sink every Friday night.

9. Drinking. Another trap for female clients of mine is being almost Paleo but drinking two glasses of wine every night and wondering why weight loss is not happening. Wine can send your blood sugar soaring, especially with no food in your system. Some of my male clients won't touch a white potato (because a caveman wouldn't eat it), but will never refuse a beer. If you're on a 30-day challenge or trying to lose weight, avoid alcohol. If you're at your goal weight, then an occasional tequila, vodka or gin mixed with fresh lime juice and soda water is a better choice.

10. Hydration. Most newly Paleo people seem not to drink enough water. Hydrate yourself with filtered or electrolyte-enhanced water, herbal teas and bone broths. Try not to drown yourself at meals though, as this inhibits stomach acid production. Sip on tea at meals and try to consume extra water a half hour before or two hours after your meals. This will also help with in-between-meal snacking urges, too.

11. Avoiding Supplements. If you've been eating a Standard American Diet, vegetarian or vegan diet then you may be suffering from nutrient deficiencies, low stomach acid or impaired liver function. For many people, the right supplements can help them get healthy much faster and with less stress than food alone. Don't get me wrong: I don't think long-term supplementation is the right answer for everyone, but for most people, taking additional support for their digestion and liver function can help with intense cravings and nutrient absorption. The recent launch of the Paleologix line by Chris Kresser and Robb Wolf is a terrific tool, or you can work with a nutritionist who is educated in both the Paleo diet and supplements. A trained professional can design a protocol to fit your specific situation.

12. Taking Too Much Fish Oil. Of the folks who take supplementation into their own hands, long-term, high-dose fish oil is another big mistake that many of my athletic clients make. High-dose fish oil can be beneficial in the short term but, over the long term, it can actually be harmful. I see a lot of gyms selling fish oil and offering that as a way to eat what you like, just redeem yourself by taking megadoses of fish oil to reduce inflammation and all will even out. I couldn't disagree more. I think fish oil can be therapeutic in a small dose over the long term but most people take it too far. Many people are taking a variety of supplements for dubious reasons such as "I read somewhere that it's good for something." Please read up on the dangers of long-term high-dose fish oil.

SUPPORT SUSTAINABLE FARMING

The farmer/activist in me cannot talk about the Paleo diet without bringing up the related issue of food sustainability. You may have read about the health benefits of eating grass-fed beef, eggs from pasture-raised chickens and other sustainably raised food products but there is also the bigger picture of social responsibility. Large-scale factory farming not only produces meat and produce which is less healthy for human consumption, but there are additional drawbacks beyond nutrition. I highly encourage you to step outside the industrial food system and seek out small-scale, sustainable food producers.

Shopping directly from your local, sustainable farmer means you are:

• Giving more of your money to the local economy

• Supporting the ethical treatment of animals and farm workers

• Maintaining diverse breeds of animals and vegetables

• Helping to support an industry which pays its workers fairly

- Encouraging the education of a new generation of farmers

- Saving fossil fuels that would otherwise be used in food transportation

- Keeping land in agriculture rather than in development

The Paleo food movement can help to make a big impact on the "food freedom" front. The next time you go to buy your 5-pound (2,270 g) package of bacon, please consider its source. Support your local, sustainable farmer whenever possible and nourish an industry that enriches the environment and our society instead of destroying it. Check out the resources below for ways to support food sustainability.

SUSTAINABLE SEAFOOD

Visit **www.montereybayaquarium.org,** the Monterey Bay Aquarium Seafood Watch © recommednations online for a guide to the most sustainable fish to eat. The list includes Arctic char, cod (U.S.-caught Pacific and Icelandic and Northeast Artic Atlantic hook-and-line), haddock, halibut (Pacific, wild-caught), mahi mahi (Atlantic, troll/pole), tuna (certain types), salmon (certain types) and Pacific sardines (wild-caught). If you want to buy online, there are some great companies, like Vital Choice and I Love Blue Sea, that are dedicated to supplying sustainable choices for seafood.

SUSTAINABLE MEATS

www.Eatwild.com (www.grasslandbeef.com) is the best way to connect with a local farmer raising pastured meats. U.S. Wellness Meats is an online company supplying sustainably farmed meat products. If you're looking for more exotic meats, check out **www.fossilfarms.com** for exotic meats and game. Those in the Boston area can check out my favorite butcher, Savenor's Market, located in both Cambridge and Boston. They happen to sell these amazing pastured eggs from a beautiful small family farm west of Boston called Clark Farm (okay, yes this is my farm) plus you'll find wild boar bacon and I even got lamb bacon there. The owner pays huge attention to detail and is very dedicated to sourcing locally.

VEGETABLES

Go to **www.localharvest.org** to connect with a vegetable C.S.A. in your area. There are some other online resources for C.S.A.s, but our farm has gotten the most new members from www.localharvest.org than any other online directory.

As you make the recipes in this book, consider the choices you can make to contribute to the sustainable food movement.

Tip: You might notice that I don't call for any boneless, skinless chicken breast in any of my recipes. I much prefer to use a high-quality whole chicken, roast it, use the meat for wraps and make a soup with the rest of the bird. It's much more economical and sustainable than buying boneless, skinless chicken breasts. Purchasing a large quantity of sustainably-raised meat and storing it in a freezer is also another smart choice.

Clark Farm

My connection to farming started in high school when I found a job selling vegetables and helping in the fields at Pike Farms in Sagaponack. I loved the work. I loved being covered in dirt and feeling completely exhausted at the end of the day. In college, I met my husband Andrew. He was an English major with a huge environmental passion; I was working toward a degree in fine arts. At age twenty-six, Andrew decided that he wanted to be a farmer and after years of study and training, he was able to do just that.

We moved to a farm just north of Boston where Andrew was hired to be the manager. We converted it to organic, started a C.S.A. and ran an education program. After the birth of our second child, I quit my marketing job at Whole Foods and took over running the busy farm stand. After ten years at that farm, we learned about a fantastic opportunity at Clark Farm, located 30 minutes west of Boston in Carlisle, Massachusettes. It had been a dairy farm for one hundred years and the owners wanted a new farming family to start a C.S.A. and education program there. In April of 2012, we moved to Clark Farm and started a new community farm.

At Clark Farm, we raise sheep, goats, chickens, ducks and pigs and grow all sorts of vegetables for our C.S.A. We rotate the sheep on fresh pasture and follow their grazing patterns with our mobile chicken coops. Our chickens eat their natural diet of grass, bugs and even mice. The pigs roam freely through the woods, digging up roots and fattening up on the oversized zucchini clubs from the vegetable patch. Our goats devour the scrub weeds and other brush that is inedible to the sheep. We use animal fertilizer to provide nutrients to the soil. It's a complete system.

Educating the public about what we are doing is critical to our mission on the farm. We work closely with the local schools to bring children to the farm all through the year. They come to see the sheep being sheared, meet the baby chicks and harvest potatoes and carrots to eat in the lunchroom at school. We want kids to have a connection with their food so that they are more likely to conserve precious farmland in the future. We employ local students to help with farm chores and also work with an international farming education program that gives interns an opportunity to stay with us in the summer and learn about sustainable agriculture.

The farm is a part of our family life. Our kids (ages seven and nine) are actively involved in the farm. They help with the chores (like collecting eggs), assist with visitor tours and enjoy fishing in the pond and building fairy houses under the trees. They're very proud of where they live and seem to have a natural instinct for things like taking care of animals and knowing when the vegetables are ready to be harvested. They spend hours playing outside and learning about the natural cycle of life. We don't humanize the animals by giving names to the ones we raise for meat. The kids understand that we take good care of the animals and they give us protein. They're both very adventurous when it comes to trying new foods and love it when I experiment in the kitchen.

Most of our products are sold directly to families in the local community using the C.S.A. model. We work with the Carlisle Public Schools to provide vegetables for school lunches. We also sell to Savenor's Market in Cambridge and Boston, and to forward-thinking restaurants like Cambridge's Craigie on Main.

Andrew works full time on the farm. I'm able to collect fresh eggs and cook them that very morning. Fresh herbs are right outside my door. Summer can be overwhelming with the abundance of vegetables available coupled with the amount of farm chores to be done, but I do my best. Sometimes when I'm on a nutrition call with a client or trying to study biochemistry, the deafening symphony of the ducks can be distracting. There are also some naughty goats that like to jump the fence and I have to stop what I'm doing and go convince them that they belong with their friends inside the fence. It's all part of living on a working farm.

I feel that the true way to follow the Paleo diet is to eat food that is produced in a sustainable way. Locally produced, high-quality vegetables and meat raised on a small-scale, integrated farm are naturally nutrient-dense and healthy. I encourage everyone on the Paleo diet to seek out a closer relationship to his or her food sources.

FIVE SUGGESTIONS FOR PALEO SUCCESS

Okay, so you've read the pitfalls. Some people immediately get it and others struggle with transitioning to the Paleo diet. Here are a few tips I use in my nutrition practice to ensure better results:

Set Realistic (or No) Goals. Yes, I did just advise no goals. That's because weighing yourself on the scale is not the best measure of how healthy you are. If you have major intestinal discomfort after each meal, then maybe your only goal should be to heal. You can't measure that with a scale or tape measure. If weight loss is your goal, please be realistic. Don't expect that, just because your friend lost 30 pounds/13 kg in one month, your body will react the same way. For some people, weight loss happens slowly and for others the weight won't come off until week three. If you are on the scale every day, you are only setting yourself up for disappointment.

Throw Stuff Out. Get rid of all non-Paleo foods in your house and stock up on tons of healthy choices. Bad decisions are made when non-Paleo food is right in front of you. Don't worry about wasting that three-year-old box of bow tie pasta sitting in the back of your cabinet. Donate it to your local food pantry or simply throw it out. I repeat, throw it out.

Indulge Yourself. Sometimes people feel deprived when they miss their old comfort foods. Add that to the winter blues that come at the time when most people start a new diet and you can easily feel defeated. Schedule massages, facials, or whatever it is that you enjoy doing just for yourself. Buy yourself a new book or enjoy some friend time and learn to treat yourself without resorting to food for comfort.

Avoid Workout Stress. Unlimited working out is a surefire way to increase hunger. Food has a much bigger part in how you look and feel than most people realize. Don't stress your system with six ten-mile runs a week. Try to include some yoga and relaxation techniques like meditation. You want to calm your body, not induce stress. Stress leads to weight gain. The other side of the coin is that I sometimes see people who change their eating and don't move at all. You should find something you enjoy doing and move on a regular basis.

Support. This comes in two forms: One is family support and the other is nutritional support. I actually suggest to people *not* to take on a new diet with a spouse. Your spouse could be your worst enemy. Yes, you both have the best intentions but when one person slips, the other usually uses this as an excuse to indulge, too. Plus, you are doing this for *you*. Take care of yourself first, and then worry about the rest of your family. If you are not committed to *you*, then it's not going to work. I know you want to help your kids, your sick aunt and your dad whose doctor just put him on cholesterol medication but the most important person who needs help right now is *you*. The second level of support I suggest having is that of a good nutritionist. They can help you tweak and balance your diet and suggest supplements to aid stress reduction and weight loss. They can analyze your cortisol levels and blood work to see if you have any imbalances and suggest foods that work best for your specific health situation and lifestyle.

STOCK UP: THE PALEO PANTRY

Here is a general idea of what I have in my kitchen. The perishable items come and go with what's available seasonally.

NON-REFRIGERATED ITEMS

Beverages: black, green and herbal teas, sustainably-sourced coffee

Cabinet staples: nuts, jerky, jarred pesto and pasta sauces, canned tomatoes, tomato paste, anchovy paste, olives, hearts of palm, artichoke hearts, sundried tomatoes, full-fat coconut milk, coconut flour, potato starch/flour, tapioca starch/flour, sustainably-sourced canned sardines, tuna, salmon and crab, chipotle chilies in adobo sauce, unsweetened coconut flakes, roasted red peppers, nori wrappers, wakame and arame seaweed, unsweetened applesauce, dried fruit, vanilla, maple syrup and local honey

Cooking fats: coconut oil, ghee, olive oil (see Frozen Items for more)

Vegetables: sweet potatoes, Yukon gold or other white potatoes, tropical roots like yucca, batata, mangala, winter squash (butternut, sweet dumpling, delicata, spaghetti, acorn) plus lots of onions and garlic

Fruit bowl: avocadoes, tomatoes, lemons, limes and seasonal fruits: citrus, apples, pears, mangoes, pineapple, melons and stone fruits

Dried herbs and spices: sea salt, black pepper, cayenne, chili powder, chipotle powder, red pepper flakes, cumin, rosemary, thyme, oregano, savory, dried onion and garlic, turmeric, curry powder, nutmeg, cardamom, cinnamon, paprika, smoked paprika, truffle oil (yes, this sounds fancy but I consider it a must-have!) and truffle-infused salt and honey

Tip: I buy my dried herbs and spices from the bulk section of my local food co-op and put them in my own containers–it's fresher and cheaper this way.

REFRIGERATED ITEMS

Beverages: water, electrolyte-enhanced water, coconut water (I also love my bubbly water machine and flavor it with fresh lemon or lime juice.), kombucha (fermented tea)

In the door: grass-fed butter (if you tolerate dairy), coconut aminos, Paleo-friendly and gluten-free condiments like barbecue sauce, Worcestershire sauce, fish sauce, chopped ginger and lemongrass, fruit-sweetened preserves, nut butters, vinegars (apple cider, balsamic, white wine, red wine, blood orange), lacto-fermented veggies like sauerkraut, pickles and kim-chee, Dijon and grainy mustard, natural sriracha (see Resources, Page 185), red Thai curry paste, salsa

Fresh seasonal vegetables: cooking greens (spinach, chard, kale, mustard, bok choy, cabbage), fresh lettuce and/or lettuce mixes, artichokes, fennel, celery, carrots, beets, zucchini, summer squash, eggplant, cucumbers, mushrooms, cauliflower, broccoli, asparagus, leeks, scallions, kohlrabi, daikon and other radishes

Fresh herbs: basil, mint, chives, tarragon, parsley, cilantro, dill

Fresh berries: whatever is in season

Cheese drawer: raw milk cheese, crème fraîche (if tolerated) and charcuterie meats (salami, prosciutto, turkey, roast beef)

Other: pasture-raised eggs, cream, fermented dairy (if tolerated), fresh, sustainable fish (wild-caught salmon for example) and thawed meat, ready to cook

FROZEN ITEMS

Frozen vegetables (I usually have frozen spinach and string beans) and berries, sustainably sourced meats like beef, pork, lamb, goat, whole chickens and ducks and game meats like venison, wild caught frozen fish and shrimp, containers of homemade broth. I also have beef bones and a few chicken carcasses in here waiting to become broth and frozen containers of bacon fat, duck fat, tallow and lard.

PALEO TO GO ALL WEEK LONG

Try this sample menu to get you started on your new "Paleo to Go" lifestyle. Planning meals ahead of time and packaging leftovers for next-day grab-and-go convenience is key to fitting this diet into your hectic schedule.

MONDAY

Breakfast: Cherry Tarragon Breakfast Sausages (page 121), fresh blueberries

Lunch: Wild Tuna, Orange and Parsley Salad (page 95)

Dinner: Pulled Pork with Orange and Herbs (page 148), Tuscan Breakfast Hash (page 141), steamed broccoli

TUESDAY

Breakfast: Curried Green Eggs and Ham (page 122)

Lunch: Pulled Pork Wrap with Sauerkraut and Avocado (page 75)

Dinner: leg of lamb, Indian-Spiced Roasted Winter Squash (page 171), sautéed spinach

WEDNESDAY

Breakfast: Bacon, Lemon and Greens Egg Muffins (page 138)

Lunch: Lamb Mango Curry Wrap (page 73)

Dinner: Salmon and Zucchini Sliders (page 159), leftover Indian-Spiced Roasted Winter Squash

THURSDAY

Breakfast: leftover Bacon, Lemon and Greens Egg Muffins

Lunch: leftover Salmon and Zucchini Sliders, side salad of baby arugula

Dinner: Moroccan Meatballs in Sweet Potato Crepes (page 74), Winter Beet Salad with Orange and Fennel (page 96)

FRIDAY

Breakfast: Blueberry Cinnamon Coconut Smoothie (page 146)

Lunch: leftover Moroccan Meatballs in Sweet Potato Crepes

Dinner: Brazilian Fish Stew (page 115)

CHAPTER 1

Grab-and-Go Paleo Wraps

These quick and delicious wraps can be made right before you jet out for your day. All you need is a few key ingredients and you've got a gourmet, simple and portable lunch that is completely grain free and good for you. You can pick up a plain roasted chicken and a few other components and assemble the Pineapple Bacon and Chicken Wrap, the Avocado, Orange and Herb Chicken Wrap, or the Lemon Chicken and Veggie Wrap in just a few minutes.

There's no need to feel deprived when deli take-out sandwiches are off limits. The Portable Tuscan Wrap and the Pastrami and Pickles in Radicchio Wrap will satisfy that craving Paleo style. The Roast Beef and Tomato Wrap with Ginger Sauce and the Roast Beef and Celeriac Slaw Wrap are truly an upgrade from your traditional roast beef sandwich.

Looking for something a little different and exotic? Try the Smoked Duck Wrap with Cherries and Hazelnuts or the Smoked Ham and Melon Wrap with Truffle Oil. There's nothing plain or ordinary about these exquisite wraps that can be made in no time and deliver extra flavor. Like the wrap contents but don't love the wrapper? No problem. Use lettuce, radicchio, sliced lunch meats, steamed chard, zucchini, grilled eggplant, or toasted nori wrappers to customize your lunch.

These grab-and-go wraps will leave you feeling full, happy and ready for anything the afternoon brings. Whether it's a big board meeting or an afternoon of shuttling kids to sports, you'll feel full and won't need to refuel until dinner. Tip: Package any of these wraps in a paper towel and then some recycled aluminum foil to help the wrap stay together as you eat and to keep the lettuce crunchy.

CHICKEN AND PEACH FIRECRACKER WRAP

This is one of my favorite wraps because of how easy, quick and absolutely delicious it is. The sauce is incredible even on its own—save some extra and use it as a dipping sauce for chicken wings! It's got heat, but the peaches cool it down. The Chicken and Peach Firecracker Wrap has it all: great protein, some good fats and incredible flavor. The best part—it only takes minutes to make.

Makes 2 large wraps (1 lunch serving)

INGREDIENTS

1 tbsp (10 g) fruit-sweetened peach preserves

1 tsp chopped hot pickled peppers

4-6 oz (112-170 g) roasted chicken breast

2 slices bacon

4 large lettuce leaves

pepper

INSTRUCTIONS

To make the sauce, combine the peach preserves with the pickled peppers. To assemble each wrap, first add half of the chicken to a large lettuce leaf. Top with half the peach sauce then 1 slice of bacon. Add a few twists of freshly ground black pepper. Cover with the second lettuce leaf. To pack for the office, wrap the entire sandwich in a paper towel then in a sheet of tinfoil.

PORTABLE TUSCAN WRAP

The next time you're walking by a deli and wishing there was something Paleo friendly to order, resolve to make this wrap. You'll feel much better avoiding bread, plus the flavors of this "sub" are much brighter than what you'd get with takeout. I decided to make a bunch of these Italian lettuce rollups for a trip to the beach one hot sunny afternoon. They tasted great, even after several hours in the cooler. Only one of the wraps came home, but I tossed it in the fridge and I ate it the next day. It was still crunchy and tasted terrific! The fat from these meats will leave you feeling satisfied for hours. Try adding other meats, like leftover roasted turkey or roast beef if you have it on hand. Also, feel free to increase the portion size.

Makes 2 sandwich wraps (1 lunch serving)

INGREDIENTS

4 romaine lettuce leaves (2 large and 2 slightly smaller leaves)

4 slices of prosciutto

4 to 6 slices of sopressata

4 to 6 slices of Genoa salami

4 to 6 slices of capocollo

2 heaping tsp basil pesto (store bought or see recipe, page 182)

6 to 8 slices (about 1" [2.5 cm] wide) of roasted red peppers

INSTRUCTIONS

To assemble each wrap, lay down a large lettuce leaf and layer 2 slices of prosciutto, then 2 to 3 slices of sopressata, salami and capocollo. Add 1 heaping teaspoon of pesto across the top and finally add the strips of red peppers. Cover with the second lettuce leaf. To pack for the office, wrap the entire sandwich in a paper towel then in a sheet of tinfoil.

CHICKEN, CELERIAC AND MUSTARD SALAD WRAP

The first time I tried this wrap, I knew it was a winner. It's a nice departure from your standard chicken salad and the good fats used in the homemade mayo are much healthier than those used in commercial chicken salad. If you happen to belong to a C.S.A. (Community Supported Agriculture) you're probably already familiar with the very ugly vegetable called celeriac. Celeriac, also called celery root, has a crunchy texture and celery flavor that blends really well with mustard. It's a great source of vitamin K and contains many antioxidants. I also love the large amount of parsley in this recipe because it contains luteolin, an antioxidant that prevents free radical damage. Parsley is also an excellent source of vitamins A, C and K. The slightly bitter but firm texture of the radicchio works great as a wrap for this amazing chicken salad.

Makes just over 1 quart (800 g) of salad

INGREDIENTS

1 large, or 2 small, head(s) of celeriac

2 cups (280 g) diced roasted chicken

¼ red onion, sliced thinly on mandoline or with knife

¾ cup (45 g) flat leaf parsley, minced

½ cup (120 g) homemade mayo (page 180)

2 cloves garlic, minced

2 tbsp (22 g) grainy mustard

1 tsp Dijon mustard

2 tbsp (30 ml) apple cider vinegar

salt and pepper to taste

2 to 4 radicchio leaves for each lunch serving

INSTRUCTIONS

With a sharp knife, remove the outer part of the celeriac. Grate, slice on a mandoline or matchstick the celeriac into long, thin pieces and put in a medium-sized bowl. Add in the chicken, parsley and red onion. In a separate bowl, combine the mayo, garlic, mustards and vinegar and mix well. Add the mayo mixture to the celeriac mixture and mix well. Salt and pepper to taste. When ready to serve, place about ⅔ cup/200 g (depending on the size of the radicchio leaf) in the leaf. Cover with another small leaf if bringing to the office. To pack for the office, wrap the entire sandwich in a paper towel then in a sheet of tinfoil.

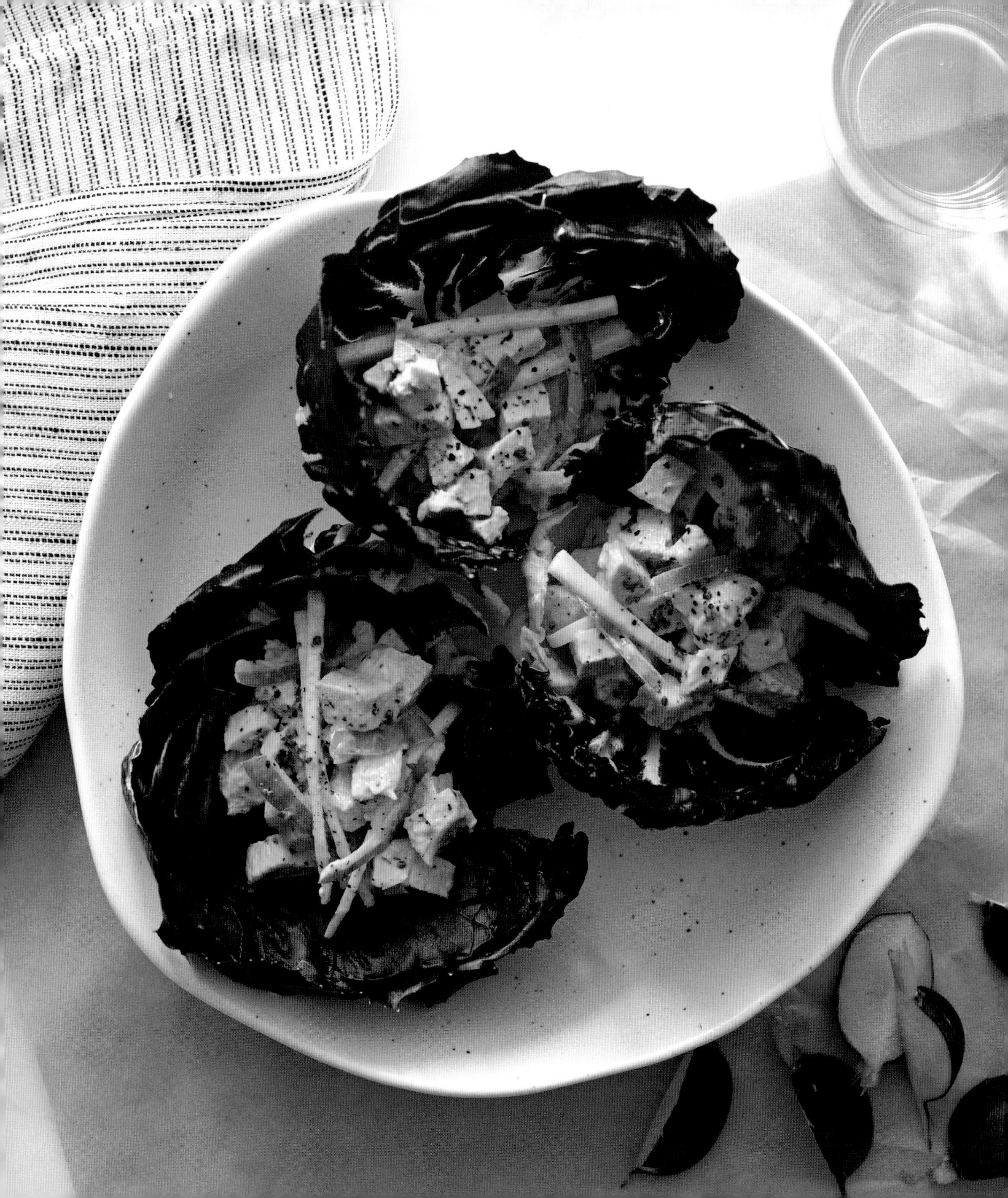

TURKEY APRICOT DIJON WRAP

I've been using a combination of apricot preserves, Dijon and thyme as a grilling sauce for years. The fruity combination goes great with turkey, chicken, pork and I also really love it on salmon. You can find apricot preserves sweetened with juice instead of sugar at most large grocery stores. This wrap is delicious and super easy to put together on a busy morning when you've got little time to spare.

Makes 2 large wraps (1 lunch serving)

INGREDIENTS

1 tbsp (10 g) fruit-sweetened apricot preserves

1 tsp fresh thyme leaves

1 tbsp (11 g) Dijon mustard

6 oz (170 g) roasted turkey

4 large leaves romaine lettuce

2 slices bacon

1 scallion, minced

INSTRUCTIONS

For the sauce, combine the apricot preserves, thyme and Dijon in a small bowl and mix well. For each wrap, layer 3 ounces (84 g) of turkey in a lettuce leaf and top with 1 slice of bacon. Spoon about 1 to 2 teaspoons of the apricot mustard sauce on each wrap, top with half of the scallion, and cover with the second lettuce leaf. Repeat for the second wrap. Roll it up, wrap it in a paper towel and tinfoil and you're off to work!

SMOKED HAM AND MELON WRAP WITH TRUFFLE OIL

Aromatic and luxurious, fast and very portable, this is a truly amazing combination. White truffle oil is available at most large grocery stores and a little goes a long way. The musky and earthy truffle flavor infuses the melon and really intensifies its flavor. I absolutely love this wrap and I know you will too! It's nice and light but keeps you full and happy for the rest of your work day.

Makes 3 wraps (1 lunch serving)

INGREDIENTS

Hassle-Free Homemade Mayonnaise (page 180)

6 romaine lettuce leaves

4 oz (112 g) smoked ham

¼ cantaloupe or similar musk melon (ripe but not overripe), peeled and sliced

¼ tsp white truffle oil

INSTRUCTIONS

For each wrap, spread a small amount of homemade mayo on a lettuce leaf. Add a third of the ham and then top with a third of the sliced melon. Drizzle about ¼ teaspoon of white truffle oil over the melon. Cover with another lettuce leaf. To pack for the office, wrap the entire sandwich in a paper towel then in a sheet of tinfoil.

BACON AND EGG WRAP WITH SUNDRIED TOMATO

Simple, portable and gourmet with the rich, deep taste of sundried tomatoes, this wrap features the aromatic and assertive flavor of fresh rosemary. If you follow my recipe for Easy-Peel Hard-Boiled Eggs (page 152), you can't go wrong. I keep rosemary plants in pots that I put outside in the summer and move indoors in the winter. If you're lucky enough to live where rosemary grows year round, consider planting some. You'll love the unique flavor it brings to your meals.

Makes 3 wraps (1 lunch serving)

INGREDIENTS

3 large lettuce leaves

2 hardboiled eggs, sliced ¼ inch (6 mm) thick

1 tbsp (7 g) sundried tomatoes packed in olive oil, minced

1 tsp fresh rosemary, minced

3 slices of bacon, cooked

pepper to taste

INSTRUCTIONS

On each lettuce leaf, place a third of the sliced egg, then a third of the sundried tomatoes and a third of the fresh rosemary. Top each wrap with one slice of bacon and some pepper.

TANGY ROAST BEEF AND BEETS WRAP

Portable, delicious and simple—this wrap has it all! I found a package of already-cooked beets in the produce section of my local specialty food store and have since noticed them at standard grocery stores. They taste great and make for speedy sandwich additions! The earthy beets paired with the slight licorice taste of the tarragon and pungent horseradish stand up well against roast beef. Three of these wraps keep me full all afternoon. Feel free to add more roast beef or beets to your wraps if you need extra fuel.

Makes 3 wraps (1 lunch serving)

INGREDIENTS

1 tbsp (14 g) Hassle-Free Homemade Mayonnaise (page 180)

1 heaping tsp prepared horseradish

1 tsp diced tarragon (if you don't like tarragon, try fresh basil, rosemary or chives instead)

6 leaves romaine lettuce

⅓ lb (151 g) thinly sliced, all-natural rare roast beef

1 red onion, thinly sliced

1 large beet, sliced thin

Salt and pepper to taste

INSTRUCTIONS

First, mix the mayo sauce by combining the mayo, horseradish and tarragon. To make each wrap, place an 8 x 8-inch (20 x 20 cm) square of tinfoil on the counter and cover it with a paper towel. Take a large slice of romaine and place it on the paper towel. Layer the roast beef, the mayo mixture, 5 to 6 thin slices of onion and finally 3 to 4 slices of beet. Add a dash of salt and pepper. Cover with another lettuce leaf. To pack for the office, roll the entire sandwich in the paper and tinfoil, and toss it in your lunch bag.

CRISP VEGGIE AND TURKEY ROLLUP

This is a great go-to wrap when I'm literally rushing out the door and need something delicious. Unlike my other wraps, which use the lettuce as the holder, this one uses the meat to hold the contents of the wrap together. Wraps like this one are filling but won't leave you feeling like an overstuffed turkey all afternoon. You'll love the dressing. I make it all of the time and keep it in the refrigerator for weeknight salads. It adds a little healthy fat to your diet in addition to great flavor.

Makes 3 wraps (1 lunch serving)

INGREDIENTS

4 oz (112 g) sliced roasted turkey

1 cup (55 g) baby salad greens (I like the mixtures with herbs added to them)

½ avocado, sliced

¼ red pepper, sliced very thin

½ carrot, peeled and shredded

¼ cucumber, peeled and seeded, sliced into matchsticks

¼ cup (10 g) radish sprouts

3 oz (90 ml) Dreamy Creamy Herb Dressing for dipping (page 184)

INSTRUCTIONS

For each wrap, first lay down one third of the turkey. Depending on how thinly sliced it is, this may be anywhere from about 2 to 4 slices. Next, add a handful of salad greens, 2 slices of avocado, a few slivers of red pepper, about 1 tablespoon (8 g) of the carrots, a few matchsticks of cucumber and one third of the sprouts. Roll it all up and secure with a toothpick. Repeat for the other two wraps. To pack for the office, plastic wrap or tinfoil works well to hold the wraps together. Pack the dressing separately and allow it to sit at room temperature for about 1 hour before eating, otherwise it will be too thick for dipping.

AVOCADO, ORANGE AND HERB CHICKEN WRAP

Packed with vitamin C, this wrap is refreshing and delicious! The longer it sits, the more the chicken picks up the orange and herb flavors, so this is a great dish to pack for the office. I love making this in the summer. It's just the thing when I get back from a midday workout at the gym and need a quick, energy-replenishing lunch. The chicken will keep you powered up for the rest of the afternoon, and the fat from the avocado will keep you full until dinner.

Makes approximately 4 large wraps (about 2 lunch servings)

INGREDIENTS

1 orange

1 avocado, cubed

1 whole chicken breast from a roasted chicken, diced (about 10 oz)

1 tbsp (2 g) fresh basil, minced

1 tsp minced mint

1 tsp minced chives

salt and pepper to taste

8 large leaves of Bibb lettuce, cleaned (if the leaves are small, just use more for the filling)

3 tbsp (15 g) toasted coconut flakes for garnish (optional)

INSTRUCTIONS

You could go to the trouble of sectioning the orange if you wish, but there's some good nutrition in that pith so you really shouldn't bother. Peel the orange and dice it into 1-inch (2.5 cm) pieces. Combine with the cubed avocado, chicken, basil, mint and chives. Add salt and pepper to taste. Serve in a nice large leaf of Bibb lettuce. To toast the coconut, simply place the coconut flakes on your toaster oven tray and toast until lightly browned. Sprinkle toasted coconut on the wrap fillings.

To pack for the office, cover with the second lettuce leaf and wrap the entire sandwich in a paper towel then in a sheet of tinfoil.

SMOKED DUCK WRAP
WITH CHERRIES AND HAZELNUTS

This wrap is quick, decadent and sure to put a huge smile on your face. I love the combination of the warm smoked duck with the sweet cherries plus a little crunch of hazelnut to top it off. You can find all-natural smoked duck at good natural food stores like Whole Foods. Duck is a nice change from other poultry and has a rich, meaty taste that I find more satiating than chicken. Other fruits like apricots and plums also pair very well with duck meat.

Makes about 3 wraps (1 lunch serving)

INGREDIENTS

4 to 6 oz (112 to 170 g) smoked duck breast

6 romaine or Boston lettuce leaves

2 tsp fruit-sweetened cherry preserves

10 hazelnuts, toasted

Freshly ground pepper

INSTRUCTIONS

Slice the duck breast into approximately ¼-inch (6 mm) slices and warm it, either in your office microwave (only about 15 seconds) or toaster oven for about 1 minute. For each wrap, place a layer of the warm sliced duck on the lettuce first, then add about ¾ teaspoon of the cherry preserves and top with one third of the chopped hazelnuts. Add a few twists of freshly ground pepper. Cover with the second lettuce leaf. To pack for the office, wrap the entire sandwich in a paper towel then in a sheet of tinfoil.

SPICY CRAB, AVOCADO AND GRAPEFRUIT NORI ROLLS

Some of the ingredients in my favorite sushi rolls are definitely not Paleo compliant, so I learned how to make my own. When you roll it yourself, you can add all kinds of fun ingredients! The grapefruit adds a nice pop to this spicy nori, and the creamy avocado mellows the whole thing out. When you switch to all-natural and non-iodized sea salt, it's a good idea to get some seaweed into your diet to avoid any potential iodine deficiency. The technique for rolling this wrap comes from Melissa Joulwan, author of *Well Fed: Paleo Recipes For People Who Love to Eat*. She came up with the clever idea of spreading the avocado across the entire sheet of nori to use it like glue to hold the roll together.

Makes 3 large rolls (1 to 2 lunch servings, depending on how hungry you are)

INGREDIENTS

2 tbsp (28 g) Hassle-Free Homemade Mayonnaise (page 180)

1 tsp sriracha (see Resources)

1 6.5 oz (182 g) can sustainable crabmeat

2 tbsp (2 g) cilantro, minced

2 tbsp (2 g) chives, minced

2 tsp mint, minced

3 toasted nori wrappers

1 avocado, sliced

8 snow peas, sliced thin lengthwise

¼ grapefruit, sectioned

4" (10 cm)-long piece daikon radish, peeled and cut into matchsticks

INSTRUCTIONS

First, make the crab salad by combining the mayo, sriracha, crab, cilantro, chives and mint in a bowl. Have all of your prepped ingredients out in front of you. Now, place a piece of nori shiny side down on a bamboo sushi mat. With about one fourth of the avocado, form a thin, single layer of slices on the nori. Leave a naked 1-inch (2.5 cm) strip on the side closest to you. Use the back of a spoon to spread the avocado across the surface of the nori. It doesn't need to cover it completely—just enough to help seal the roll and soften the nori. Repeat with the 2 remaining nori sheets. Now, place the crab salad in the "naked" part of the nori. Next, make a parallel strip of snow peas on top of the avocado, then another strip of daikon on top of the snow peas, and finally a layer of the grapefruit over that. Carefully roll the sushi from the crab side, going slowly. At the end, give the roll a little squeeze to help the avocado hold it all together. Slice in half, then in half again and again until you have 8 uniform pieces of sushi. Repeat with the other 2 rolls. Carefully pack the sliced rolls into a container so they're pretty cozy, that way they'll stay together.

Tip: To keep the avocado from turning brown, sprinkle the roll with some fresh lemon juice.

TURKEY APPLE BACON WRAP
WITH LEMON HERB SAUCE

There's nothing plain or boring about this turkey wrap. The tarragon chive lemon sauce makes the turkey, which some people find bland, pop with flavor. This wrap is bursting with crisp, sweet apples and it offers a bite of salty bacon that I know you'll love. If you aren't a fan of tarragon, feel free to substitute fresh rosemary or basil or add some curry powder to the mayo to spice it up. I use a bit more mayo on this sandwich than on my others, simply because real roasted turkey breast tends to be dry.

Makes 2 large wraps (1 lunch serving)

INGREDIENTS

FOR THE SAUCE:

1 tbsp (14 g) Hassle-Free Homemade Mayonnaise (page 180)

1 tbsp (2 g) fresh tarragon, minced

1 tsp fresh chives, minced

1 tsp lemon

salt and pepper to taste

FOR THE WRAP:

4 romaine lettuce leaves

6 oz (170 g) sliced roasted turkey

½ apple, peeled and sliced thin

2 to 4 bacon slices

INSTRUCTIONS

To make the sauce, simply combine the mayo with the herbs and lemon, and then add a pinch of salt and a little pepper. For each wrap, lay down a large lettuce leaf and cover with 1 layer of turkey. Add a bit of the mayo on top of the turkey, and then add a layer of sliced apples and bacon. Add another layer of mayo before adding a second layer of turkey and, finally, top with the smaller lettuce leaf. Wrap the entire sandwich in a paper towel then tinfoil before heading out the door.

LEMON, CHIVE, BEET AND BOILED EGG WRAP

Here's a simple wrap with earthy flavors that also happens to be vegetarian. If you're short on time, you can find already roasted beets in the produce section of most grocery stores, but I also really enjoy roasting beets myself. Beets come in many colors, from deep red to yellow and even striped. They are a good source of starch and contain lots of vitamins and minerals, like folate and manganese. Roasting beets is very simple: You just pierce them a few times with a knife, drizzle with a tiny bit of melted coconut oil, and wrap in tinfoil. Roast them in a 350°F (176°C) oven for about 1 hour or until they are soft in the middle.

Makes 3 wraps (about 1 lunch serving)

INGREDIENTS

FOR THE SAUCE:

1 tbsp (14 g) Hassle-Free Homemade Mayonnaise (page 180)

1 tsp fresh lemon juice

1 tbsp (1 g) fresh chives, minced

FOR THE WRAP:

6 large romaine lettuce leaves

9 to 12 fresh basil leaves

2 pasture-raised hard-boiled eggs, sliced ¼" (6 mm) thick (get yourself an egg slicer for the best results)

3 small or 1 large beet, cooked, skinned and sliced

salt and pepper to taste

INSTRUCTIONS

To make the sauce, combine the mayo, lemon juice and chives in a small bowl. Set aside. Lay out the lettuce leaves and start by placing one third of the basil leaves in the lettuce, followed by one third of the sliced egg, 1 teaspoon of the mayo and one third of the sliced beets. Top with a sprinkle of salt and pepper. Cover with the second lettuce leaf. To pack for the office, wrap the entire sandwich in a paper towel then in a sheet of tinfoil.

CHICKEN CRANBERRY SALAD AND FENNEL WRAP

This chicken salad is always a big hit, and it's so much healthier (and more delicious) than deli chicken salad that is made with bad oils. If you think you don't like fennel or you've never tried it, taste this dish and see how amazing it can be. Fennel has been used since ancient times for relief from anemia, indigestion and respiratory disorders among other illnesses. In Italy, they use fennel like Americans use celery. I think that fennel is much more interesting for its texture and how it can make dishes pop. To make this wrap quickly and easily, I use the meat left over from a free-range roasted chicken, but you can also pick up a roasted chicken in the deli case. Look for roasted chickens that have no added chemicals, as the list can be long! The dried cranberries provide a nice pop of flavor and vitamin C. Be careful to seek out dried cranberries that are unsweetened, as many brands are sweetened with sugar or fruit juice.

Makes about 4 servings

INGREDIENTS

3 to 4 cups (420 to 560 g) cooked and cubed chicken

1 bulb fennel, minced

½ cup (75 g) roasted cashews, unsalted

½ cup (60 g) dried cranberries

2 tbsp (28 g) Hassle-Free Homemade Mayonnaise (page 180)

1 tsp dried sage

2 tbsp (8 g) fresh parsley

salt and pepper to taste

8 romaine lettuce leaves

INSTRUCTIONS

Simply mix all of the ingredients except the lettuce in a bowl. When ready to serve, spoon the chicken salad into the lettuce leaves. To pack for the office, bring chicken salad in a separate container and spoon into the lettuce leaves when you're ready to eat.

ROAST BEEF AND CELERIAC SLAW WRAP

This delicious slaw takes only a few minutes to make. It's excellent on its own but also goes great with rare, high quality roast beef. The lemon and tarragon give the slaw a fresh, bright taste while the crisp celeriac is a good source of vitamin B6, magnesium, manganese, and an excellent source of vitamin C, vitamin K, phosphorus and potassium. Look for celeriac in the refrigerated section of the produce department near the carrots and celery.

Makes 2 large wraps (enough for 1 serving)

INGREDIENTS

FOR THE SLAW:

1 cup (110 g) peeled and shredded celeriac

1 tbsp (2 g) tarragon, minced

2 tbsp (28 g) Hassle-Free Homemade Mayonnaise (page 180)

1 tsp minced horseradish

1 tsp fresh lemon juice

salt and pepper to taste

FOR THE WRAP:

⅓ lb (151 g) roast beef

4 large leaves Boston lettuce

INSTRUCTIONS

Remove the outer skin of the celeriac and slice it on a mandoline. To make the slaw, combine the celeriac, tarragon, mayo, horseradish and lemon juice. Add a dash of salt and a few shakes of pepper. Combine well. For each wrap, place half of the roast beef on the lettuce and top with the slaw. Cover the slaw with the second lettuce leaf. To pack for the office, wrap the entire sandwich in a paper towel then in a sheet of tinfoil.

LEMON CHICKEN AND VEGGIE WRAP

This crisp and refreshing wrap is a great break from your dense, slow cooker leftovers. Don't let the radish scare you. It's got a great crunch and a little bite that adds texture and flavor to many wraps and salads. To keep radishes fresher longer, chop the tops off and keep them in a bag in your refrigerator. I've had some last months in the crisper drawer! There are many different varieties of radishes. Try the long and skinny D'Avignon radish, the mellow daikon, or the beautiful Easter egg radish in shades of red and purple.

Makes 3 wraps (1 lunch serving)

INGREDIENTS

1 tbsp (14 g) Hassle-Free Home-made Mayonnaise (page 180)

½ tsp fresh lemon juice

4 to 6 oz (112 to 170 g) roasted chicken breast

¼-½ cucumber, peeled and thinly sliced

2 radishes, sliced thin on a mandoline or with a sharp knife

1 tbsp (2 g) fresh mint, minced

1 tbsp (2 g) fresh basil, minced

3 Boston lettuce leaves

Pinch of salt and pepper

INSTRUCTIONS

Combine the lemon juice and mayo. For each wrap, layer a third of the chicken on the lettuce and then add 1 teaspoon of the lemon mayo. Top with a third of the cucumbers, radishes and fresh herbs. Sprinkle with salt and pepper. Repeat for the other 2 wraps. Cover them with the second lettuce leaf. To pack for the office, wrap the entire sandwich in a paper towel then in a sheet of tinfoil.

PINEAPPLE BACON AND CHICKEN WRAP

This wrap is so delicious, sweet and tangy. Okay so I can't think of many things that don't go with bacon, but pineapple was just made for bacon! A touch of barbecue sauce mixed in with homemade mayonnaise gives this wrap a slightly sweet tang. Your mouth will be very, very happy! The best part is, it's a great healthy alternative to gooey, syrupy barbecue sandwiches that Joe over in the corner cube is wolfing down with an extra-large soda. You'll be satisfied and sharp all afternoon long.

Makes 3 wraps (1 lunch serving)

INGREDIENTS

1 tbsp (14 g) Hassle-Free Homemade Mayonnaise (page 180)

1 tbsp (14 g) your favorite gluten-free barbecue sauce (see Resources)

1 tsp lime juice

Salt and pepper to taste

½ roasted chicken breast (about 4 oz [112 g])

6 Boston lettuce leaves

½ cup (80 g) sliced fresh pineapple

2 slices bacon, crumbled

2 tsp fresh chives, minced

INSTRUCTIONS

To make the sauce, combine the mayo with the barbecue sauce and lime juice. Add salt and pepper to taste. To make the wraps, start by placing the chicken in a large leaf of lettuce. Top it with a teaspoon of the sauce, then the pineapple and finally sprinkle on the bacon and chives. Cover with the second lettuce leaf. To pack for the office, wrap the entire sandwich in a paper towel then in a sheet of tinfoil.

ROAST BEEF AND TOMATO WRAP
WITH GINGER SAUCE

What a simple and amazing combination! The first time I heard of pairing ginger and tomato, I wasn't convinced. All I can say is *wow*! Fresh ginger gives this wrap a warm, fresh feel and transforms these familiar ingredients into a unique and exciting lunch. The trick with fresh tomatoes in a lettuce wrap is to keep them separated from the lettuce using the meat as a barrier. This keeps the lettuce from getting soggy. When you pack this delicious wrap in your lunchbox, the tomato and ginger mingle together, flavoring the roast beef. At lunch, these flavors explode in your mouth. Yeah, it's that good!

Makes 3 wraps (1 lunch serving)

INGREDIENTS

1 tbsp (14 g) Hassle-Free Homemade Mayonnaise (page 180)

1 tsp freshly grated ginger

4 to 6 oz (112 to 170 g) rare and thinly sliced roast beef

6 large romaine lettuce leaves

3 thin slices of red onion

1 tomato, sliced (try an heirloom like Brandywine)

INSTRUCTIONS

For the sauce, mix the mayo with the fresh ginger. For each wrap, lay a third of the roast beef on the lettuce first. On one half of the beef, place the onion, tomato and about 1 teaspoon of the ginger sauce. Fold the other half of the roast beef over so that it is covering the tomato and mayo sauce. Cover with the second lettuce leaf. To pack for the office, wrap the entire sandwich in a paper towel then in a sheet of tinfoil.

PASTRAMI AND PICKLES
IN RADICCHIO WRAP

For those of you who miss a good pastrami-on-rye sandwich, this one is pretty amazing!
I love how the tangy pickles and pungent grainy mustard play off each other. The warm pastrami works nicely with the bitter and crunchy radicchio wrap. You also get the benefit of good bacteria from live cultured pickles, which makes this lunch especially nutritious. No need to pick up a deli sandwich anymore. This wrap is not only healthier for you, but it will also leave you feeling warm and satisfied all afternoon. On top of all this, the artist in me loves the colors of this wrap. It's beautiful, delicious and nutritious.

Makes 2 wraps (1 lunch serving)

INGREDIENTS

6 slices of pastrami

6 slices of lacto-fermented pickles*

2 tbsp (22 g) grainy mustard

2 tbsp (4 g) minced parsley

2 large leaves of radicchio

INSTRUCTIONS

For each wrap, place a leaf of radicchio on a plate. Add 1 tablespoon (2 g) of parsley, 1 tablespoon (11 g) of mustard, and 3 round slices of pickles to the lettuce. In a microwave, place the pastrami on a plate and cover with a paper towel. Heat for 30 seconds. (You can also warm the pastrami in a toaster oven if you prefer.) Top the sandwich with the warm pastrami. To pack this, pack the radicchio and dressings in a separate container from the pastrami, since you'll be heating it at the office.

Buy pickles you find in the perishable section, not the shelf-stable kind in the grocery section that are brined in vinegar. I'm talking about real, lacto-fermented pickles made with salt and water. Ask your produce manager or dairy manager to help you find them.

ZUCCHINI, PROSCIUTTO AND BASIL PINWHEELS

Need something special to go along with that soup you're packing for the office?
These little mouthfuls of flavor are lemony and a little salty from the prosciutto. They're simple
enough to make for a weekday lunch, but cute enough to serve at a party. Every time I serve
them up at a gathering, they are everyone's favorite. People swear there are more ingredients
in them than there actually are. You'll appreciate how quick and fun they are to make
for the office and how popular they'll be at your next event.

Makes about 25 bite-sized pieces

INGREDIENTS

2 zucchini

8 oz (228 g) thinly sliced prosciutto

1 bunch fresh basil

1 lemon

INSTRUCTIONS

With a mandoline, slice the zucchini lengthwise. Lay the prosciutto on a plate and place half a slice of the prosciutto along the length of the zucchini, then top with 2 to 3 leaves of fresh basil. Roll up and secure with a toothpick. When you've done them all, squeeze a lemon over the top, just to moisten and add some zest. To pack them for the office, fill a food storage container with them and bring half a lemon with you to the office to squeeze on just before eating. If you're serving them at a party, you can use the lemon half for people to put their old toothpicks in.

COSMOPOLITAN TURKEY SALAD AND PEAR WRAP

With its blend of tarragon, lemon, radishes and pears, this wrap is a welcome change from standard turkey salad. It transforms your average leftover roasted turkey into a lively and upbeat lunch that I know you'll enjoy. It's fresh and light and so much healthier for you than turkey salad from a standard deli. You'll love the blend of lemon, anise and pear flavors with the crunch of celery and radishes.

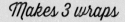

Makes 3 wraps

INGREDIENTS

1 cup (140 g) cooked and diced turkey

¼ cup (56 g) Hassle-Free Homemade Mayonnaise (page 180)

½ pear, peeled and diced

1 tsp fresh tarragon, minced

½ cup (30 g) parsley, minced

1 stalk celery, diced

1 red radish, diced

½ tsp fresh lemon juice

salt and pepper to taste

3 large leaves Boston lettuce

INSTRUCTIONS

Combine all ingredients except lettuce in a bowl. Salt and pepper to taste. Just before serving, wrap some salad in a Boston lettuce leaf. When bringing to the office, pack the turkey salad in a separate container and scoop into a lettuce leaf right before eating.

TURKEY AVOCADO AND SPICY PEPPER WRAP

This wrap is like happy fireworks in your mouth! The inspiration for this sandwich comes from Justin, my trainer at CrossFit Woodshed. I asked him what his favorite sandwich was, and this one quickly came to mind. Now I know why: The pickles, spicy peppers, and honey mustard sauce are a perfect combination of sweet, salty and spicy. Feel free to add as many pickles or peppers as you like. I prefer getting my turkey at a deli that roasts actual turkey breast, instead of buying from a company that molds it into a large, round, processed protein ball.

Makes 2 wraps (1 lunch serving)

INGREDIENTS

FOR THE SAUCE:

2 tbsp (28 g) Hassle-Free Homemade Mayonnaise (page 180)

½ tsp Worcestershire sauce (see Resources)

1 tsp honey

1 tsp Dijon mustard

FOR THE WRAP:

4 large romaine lettuce leaves

6 oz (170 g) sliced roasted turkey

2 tbsp (30 g) chopped lacto-fermented pickles

¼ avocado, sliced

2 tsp chopped spicy peppers

INSTRUCTIONS

Combine the mayo, Worcestershire sauce, honey and Dijon mustard to make the honey mustard sauce. For each wrap, lay down a lettuce leaf and place half of your sliced turkey in the wrap first, then add half of the pickles, half of the avocado, and finally 1 teaspoon of the honey mustard sauce. Finish with 1 teaspoon of the spicy peppers. Cover with the second lettuce leaf. To pack for the office, wrap the entire sandwich in a paper towel then in a sheet of tinfoil.

CHAPTER 2

Cook-and-Run Paleo Wraps

If you've been eating a Paleo diet for a while, I know you're used to leftovers for lunch. The good news is, leftovers don't have to be boring. Some of my favorite wraps incorporate slow-cooked meats or grilled vegetables from the night before. The Pulled Pork Wrap with Sauerkraut and Avocado is a great example of this. You can even transform last night's grilled fish into the Cajun Fish Po' Boy Wrap and have a lunch you won't forget. Did you have some of my Home-made Chorizo Sausage with your breakfast yesterday? Try the Mexican Chorizo Tacos today for lunch.

The key to a delicious Paleo-to-go lunch is preparation. If you dedicate a little time on the weekend or on a weeknight to cooking some of the ingredients in these warm wraps, you'll have plenty of healthy lunches to pack for days to come. A little bit of prep time is worth it when you can enjoy a workday meal like Spicy Lobster Boats, Grilled Eggplant Rollups or the Spicy Shrimp Salad Wrap.

I'm a huge fan of ethnic foods, so here I have included some of my very favorite combinations. Do you love lamb as much as I do? Try the Lamb "Dosa" Purses with Coconut Crème, a dish that I served to one hundred people at the sustainable feast at my farm last summer. It got rave reviews! The Lamb Tzatziki Gyros in Coconut Crepes and Lamb Mango Curry Wrap have exotic and exciting flavor combinations that I just can't wait for you to experience. I also love the Cinnamon Beef in a Sweet Potato Pocket and the Chinese Ginger Pork Wrap. Even if you're stuck at your desk, you'll feel like you're traveling far away on a flavor journey.

ROASTED CHICKEN, DELICATA SQUASH AND BACON WRAP

This comfort food combo can be assembled in minutes with a leftover batch of Roasted Delicata Squash, a little bacon and some chicken. It's incredibly satisfying. There will be no afternoon energy slump with this lunch. The delicata provides some good starch and vitamins without excessive calories. The bacon is delicious as always and provides healthy fats that will help keep you full until dinnertime. This wrap has a little heat, but the sweetness of the roasted squash balances it out nicely. I love this wrap in the fall when the weather is crisp and delicata squash are in season. If you can't find delicata, you can easily make it with butternut squash.

Makes 3 wraps (1 lunch serving)

INGREDIENTS

⅔ cup (168 g) Roasted Delicata Squash (page 176)

3 slices bacon

4 to 6 oz (112 to 170 g) roasted chicken breast

pepper

3 romaine or Boston lettuce leaves

INSTRUCTIONS

For each wrap, use the chicken as your base, then cover it with one third of the roasted delicata squash and top with bacon and pepper. If bringing to the office, pack the lettuce separately from the filling. When you're ready for lunch, warm the filling and stuff it into the crisp lettuce leaves.

SPICY SHRIMP SALAD WRAP

This vibrant, tropical lunch wrap is a complete Paleo meal that will leave you feeling refreshed and energetic all afternoon. This wrap is full of nutritious elements: Shrimp is a rich source of tryptophan and selenium. The avocados in this wrap provide good fats and the pineapple packs vitamin A, vitamin C, calcium, phosphorus and potassium, plus it has bromelain, which aids in digestion. If you've never tried jicama, give it a shot. It gives the salad a nice crunch.

Makes about 3 lunch servings

INGREDIENTS

1 tbsp (14 g) coconut oil

1 lb (454 g) thawed wild Maine shrimp, or thawed all natural shrimp, tail removed and cut in half

1 tsp or more of red pepper flakes, to taste

1 avocado, diced

1 cup (130 g) diced jicama (substitute daikon radish if you like)

1 cup (165 g) diced fresh pineapple

3 tbsp (3 g) fresh cilantro, minced

Juice from 1 lime

salt and pepper to taste

6 romaine lettuce leaves, washed and dried

INSTRUCTIONS

In a skillet over medium-high heat, melt the coconut oil then add the shrimp and red pepper flakes. Cook, stirring constantly for about 5 minutes, or until the shrimp are completely done. Remove from heat. In a large bowl, add the cooked shrimp, avocado, jicama, pineapple, cilantro, lime, salt and pepper to taste. Toss well. For best results, assemble these wraps right before eating them. If you are taking them to work, place the shrimp mixture in a separate container and wrap the lettuce leaves in paper towel. Allow 2 lettuce leaves and about 2 cups (230 g) of shrimp salad per person, depending on individual needs.

Tip: If you can find them, wild Maine shrimp are a more sustainable choice for this recipe than gulf or Thai farmed shrimp. Maine shrimp are smaller and can be more expensive, but they have a richer taste. If you can't find them, look for shrimp that do not contain preservatives.

CINNAMON BEEF IN A SWEET POTATO POCKET

Aromatic and warm, this amazing beef dish is one I give to my new clients as a great alternative to burgers. When I've got some grass-fed ground beef thawed in my fridge, I like to make a double batch of this recipe so my husband and I can eat it for breakfast and lunch during the week. The sweet potato crepes are like warm, nutrient-dense tortillas. If you've never tried Swiss chard before, you've been missing out on one of my favorite greens! It tastes sort of like spinach, but with a more pleasing texture. It's packed full of lots of vitamins, especially A, C and K. It's also rich in minerals like magnesium, iron, potassium and manganese.

Makes enough for 4 servings

INGREDIENTS

1 lb (454 g) grass-fed ground beef

½ white onion, chopped

3 cloves garlic, minced

½ tsp cinnamon

½ tsp ground cloves

1 tsp curry powder

1 tsp dried thyme

1 red bell pepper, diced

5 leaves Swiss chard, diced (about 1 small bunch)

1 tbsp (15 ml) coconut aminos (or wheat-free tamari)

Red pepper flakes to taste (I use about ⅛ tsp)

2 tbsp (2 g) cilantro, minced

12 Sweet Potato Crepes with Chives (page 157)

INSTRUCTIONS

Warm a large skillet on the stove and brown the ground beef. Add onion, garlic, herbs and spices. Cook until onion is soft. Add the red pepper and chard and cook for another 5 minutes. Right before serving, add the coconut aminos, cilantro and red pepper flakes. Serve about ⅓ cup of filling per sweet potato crepe. If bringing to work, pack in a separate container and warm before placing in warm sweet potato crepes. You can also serve these in crisp lettuce if you wish.

SPICY LOBSTER BOATS

This is the best lobster salad I've ever had. It's bright and beaming with fresh flavor and heat. I got the idea for this wrap from a visit to one of my favorite cafés, Grassy Roots in Wenham, Massachusetts. I decided to order something different than my usual meat-topped salad. They had some beautiful-looking lobster salad in the case so I asked them to fill a couple of romaine lettuce leaves with it. It was not only delicious but kept me feeling full all afternoon. I decided to make these a bit less messy and more manageable by stuffing them in smaller leaves using endives instead of romaine. Watch your market for lobster prices to go down; the prices can really fluctuate quite a bit depending on the season. Shrimp or crabmeat could be substituted here if lobster is too expensive or not available.

Makes about 1 quart (600 g) (enough for about 2 to 3 lunch servings)

INGREDIENTS

½ cup (120 g) Hassle-Free Homemade Mayonnaise (page 180)

⅓ cup (40 g) diced celery (about 2 sticks)

2 tbsp (2 g) fresh chives, minced

2 scallions, chopped small

2 to 3 tsp chipotle peppers in adobo sauce, minced*

½ to 1 tsp jalapeno pepper, minced (depending on your tolerance for heat)

1 tbsp (2 g) fresh basil, minced

1 tbsp (1 g) cilantro

2 tsp fresh lime juice

2 cups (240 g) lobster meat (leftovers from one large lobster)

salt and pepper to taste

2 heads of endives

INSTRUCTIONS

In a large bowl, combine the mayo with the celery, chives, scallions, chipotle, jalapeno, basil, cilantro and lime juice. Mix well. Fold in the lobster meat until well combined. Add salt and pepper to taste. Scoop about 2 tablespoons (28 g) worth of mixture into an endive leaf and repeat. If packing for the office, simply put the lobster salad in a container and bring the endives with you and fill right before you are ready to eat. This lobster salad is also excellent over a simple bed of arugula.

I've noticed a big difference in heat depending on the brand of chipotles and variety of jalapeno you purchase. Some are so much spicier than others. Start off by adding less and increase to your taste.

CAJUN FISH PO' BOY WRAP

I thought it would be fun to put a Paleo twist on this Cajun classic. When combined, the spicy and sour remoulade, peppery watercress and refreshing slice of onion make this wrap a complete winner! It's full of protein, good fats and a little starch from the wrap. Feel free to substitute crisp lettuce leaves for the coconut crepe. See page 21 for a list of sustainable options for white fish to use in this recipe.

Makes 2 lunch servings

INGREDIENTS

FOR THE FISH:
½ lb (227 g) grilled firm white fish (whatever is the most sustainable choice at the market)

½ tsp Cajun seasoning

Dash salt and pepper

½ lime

FOR THE REMOULADE:
1 clove garlic, minced

1 tbsp (15 g) minced pickle plus 1 tbsp (15 ml) pickle juice (lacto-fermented pickles recommended)

1 tsp Dijon mustard

1 tsp hot sauce (a clean brand such as Tabasco)

½ tsp thyme

1 tsp lemon juice

½ tsp cayenne pepper

½ tsp paprika

FOR THE WRAP:
6 Coconut Crepes (page 137)

12 thin slices tomato

1 cup (55 g) watercress

¼ red onion, thinly sliced

INSTRUCTIONS

Season the fish with the Cajun seasoning, salt and pepper. Grill for 10 minutes or until cooked through. Remove from heat and squeeze lime over the fish as it cools. Now make the remoulade: Simply combine the garlic, pickle, pickle juice, mustard, hot sauce, thyme, lemon juice, cayenne pepper and paprika in a bowl. For each wrap, place about 3 tablespoons (42 g) of the fish with 2 tomato slices, some watercress and a little red onion and about 1 teaspoon of the remoulade in a coconut crepe. If bringing these to the office, I suggest assembling right before you eat them. Coconut Crepes reheat very nicely.

GRILLED EGGPLANT ROLLUPS

In this wrap, the grilled eggplant is the vehicle for the salty and sweet flavors of sardines and sundried tomatoes. Toss some extra eggplant on the grill for dinner and use it to assemble these quick and easy wraps in the morning before work. Roasted eggplant can also be used. Sardines are a Paleo power food because they are an excellent source of calcium and omega-3s. I like to buy Pacific sardines packed in olive oil and lemon (see Resources).

Makes 3 to 4 rollups (1 serving)

INGREDIENTS

1 large Italian eggplant
1 tbsp (18 g) salt
1 tsp fennel seeds
1 tsp dried rosemary
1 tbsp (15 ml) olive oil
1 tsp thyme
9 leaves of fresh basil
¼ red onion, sliced very thin
9 sundried tomatoes
1 can (4.3 oz, or 120 g) sardines
Pinch of red pepper flakes (optional)

INSTRUCTIONS

Slice the eggplant about ½-inch (1.3 cm) thick lengthwise. Lay out the eggplant slices (you only need 3 to 4 per serving) on a baking sheet and sprinkle with salt on both sides. Allow to sit for about 30 minutes as the salt pulls the moisture from the eggplant. Meanwhile, grind the fennel and rosemary with a mortar and pestle so they are a bit smaller. With a paper towel, remove the excess salt and moisture from the eggplant. Drizzle with olive oil and sprinkle with the thyme, fennel and rosemary. Grill or roast the eggplant at 350°F (180°C, or gas mark 4) until light brown. To assemble each wrap, lay down a slice of eggplant then add the fresh basil for the first layer. Cover the basil with the thinly sliced onion, then the sundried tomatoes and finally, a sardine. Add a pinch of red pepper flakes if you wish. Roll up and use toothpicks to hold together. These make excellent wraps for lunch or you can serve this as an appetizer using smaller slices of eggplant. For the office, roll into tinfoil and pack in a cooler bag or store in your office fridge until you're ready for lunch. Serve with a nice green salad, if you like.

LAMB "DOSA" PURSES
WITH COCONUT CRÈME

These spicy little packets are to die for! The inspiration for these comes from my friends at Chive Sustainable Event Design and Catering, the company that prepared the food for a sustainable feast event I hosted on my farm. I've changed the recipe slightly by adding sweet potato. I thought sweet potato would make them more dosa-like while adding a little healthy starch. What resulted are these perfect Paleo packets to eat on the go. This recipe takes a bit longer to make than the others, but believe me it is completely worth your time. If you don't want to wrap them in Swiss chard, then serve them over arugula and drizzle with the coconut crème. Goat, pork or beef can also be substituted for the lamb.

Makes about 30 bite-sized wraps (3 large servings)

INGREDIENTS

FOR THE MEATBALLS:

1 large or two small sweet potatoes

1 lb (454 g) ground lamb

3 tbsp (6 g) fresh mint, minced

½ yellow onion, chopped into ¼" (6 mm) dice

3 cloves garlic, minced

1 tsp cumin

1 tsp coriander

½ tsp turmeric

¼ tsp cayenne pepper (add a little less or omit if you don't want them spicy)

¼ tsp cardamom

1 tsp fresh ginger, minced

½ tsp pepper

½ tsp salt

FOR THE WRAP:

30 Swiss chard leaves for wrappers (medium-sized is best)

1 pkg toothpicks

FOR THE COCONUT CRÈME:

½ cup (120 ml) full-fat coconut milk

1 tsp turmeric

½ tsp cardamom

¼ lime, juiced

INSTRUCTIONS

Peel and cut sweet potatoes into 2-inch (5 cm) squares; boil until done, about 15 minutes. While they are boiling, add the remaining ingredients to a bowl and preheat the oven to 425°F (220°C, or gas mark 7). Drain the water and with a potato masher, mash them until they are still slightly lumpy but mostly mashed. Add the potatoes to the lamb mixture and use your hands to mix well. On a large baking sheet lined with parchment paper, form little oblong balls—sort of like mini hot dogs. Bake for about 7 to 10 minutes or until light brown. Remove from oven and allow to cool. While the meatballs are cooling, boil a large pot of water. Blanch the Swiss chard leaves for 2 to 3 minutes and remove and place in a bowl of ice water.

To roll, take 1 leaf of Swiss chard and dry it off. Remove the stem at the bottom. Place a meatball in the leaf and roll the bottom part up, then fold over the sides, tucking in as you go, and continue to roll until the meatball is covered with the leaf. Hold in place with a toothpick. Continue until the rest are rolled.

To make the crème, mix together all of the ingredients. The result is a refreshing, aromatic sauce. It's also a terrific salad dressing, especially over roasted lamb and arugula.

LAMB MANGO CURRY WRAP

I really, really adore this simple wrap. It's sweet from the mango and warm from the curry sauce. This wrap is the perfect use for leftover roasted lamb. It's too bad that Americans only eat about 1 pound (454 g) of lamb a year. I think I must eat enough for the entire Boston metro area! Lamb meat has a sweet taste and is very tender. It can be expensive compared to subsidized, industrially raised beef, which probably explains why it's less popular than beef. On our farm, we breed our own sheep and rotate them on fresh pasture regularly. Our lamb meat is so delicious that it is the first to fly out of our freezer case when we bring it back from the butcher.

Makes 3 wraps (1 lunch serving)

INGREDIENTS

1 tbsp (14 g) Hassle-Free Homemade Mayonnaise (page 180)

1 tsp curry powder

½ tsp fresh lime juice

4 to 6 oz (112 to 170 g) roasted leg of lamb, sliced

3 large romaine lettuce leaves

¼ mango, peeled and sliced

1 tbsp (1 g) minced cilantro

1 tbsp (10 g) minced red onion

Dash salt and pepper

Pinch of red pepper flakes (optional)

INSTRUCTIONS

To make the curry mayo, combine the homemade mayo with the curry powder and lime juice. Warm the lamb. For each wrap, first place one third of the lamb in a lettuce leaf. Top with a teaspoon of the curry mayo, then add one third each of the mango, cilantro and red onion. Add a sprinkle of salt and pepper, and red pepper flakes if you wish.

MOROCCAN MEATBALLS
IN SWEET POTATO CREPES

These exotic and simple wraps can transport you right from your desk to a different world. These moist lamb meatballs have a sweet spiciness to them from the cloves and other spices. They can be cooked for a weeknight dinner and the leftovers can be transformed into this amazing sandwich. You'll never want a classic meatball sub again! You can use store-bought sauce for this wrap, such as Seggiano Red Pesto Sauce, an amazing sauce that contains no dairy and is cashew based. If you want to make your own delicious tomato sauce in a blender, see the recipe on page 166.

Makes 3 wraps (1 serving)

INGREDIENTS

9 Moroccan Meatballs (page 162)

3 Sweet Potato Crepes with Chives, (page 157)

1 tbsp (15 g) red pesto sauce, such as Seggiano Red Pesto Sauce

6 thin slices tomato

Handful of thin sliced red onion

1 tsp fresh cilantro

½ cup (26 g) baby arugula

salt and pepper to taste

INSTRUCTIONS

Warm the crepes and meatballs. For each crepe, spread about 1 teaspoon of the red pesto sauce on the crepe, then place 3 meatballs, 2 slices of tomato, a few slices of red onion, a sprinkle of cilantro and one third of the arugula. Add a pinch of salt and a dash of pepper. Repeat for the other 2 wraps.

If bringing to the office, pack the meatballs and sauce in one container and the crepes and toppings in a separate container. You'll want to warm the meatballs and sweet potato crepes in your office microwave or toaster oven. On a plate, assemble all of the ingredients as directed in the paragraph above. Enjoy!

PULLED PORK WRAP WITH SAUERKRAUT AND AVOCADO

This is one of my all-time favorite lunches! Warm pulled pork is incredibly comforting and soaks up the slightly sour flavor of the sauerkraut really well. The crepes are warm and help pull together all of the flavors into a complete package. Sauerkraut is a Paleo super food. It's not only rich in vitamins but it's also full of probiotics, those beneficial microbes that live in your guts. I love making my own, but there are lots of little companies popping up all over making traditional lacto-fermented sauerkraut like Wildbrine and Real Pickles brand. I'm so glad this ancient and nourishing food is now becoming so popular!

Makes 3 wraps (about 1 lunch serving)

INGREDIENTS

3 Coconut Crepes (page 137) or Sweet Potato Crepes (page 157)

4 to 6 oz (112 to 170 g) Pulled Pork with Orange and Herbs (page 148)

3 tbsp (26 g) Sauerkraut Made Simple (page 183)

¼-½ Avocado

INSTRUCTIONS

To make the sandwiches, prepare the Coconut Crepes or try the Sweet Potato Crepes. Into each crepe, place about 2 to 3 ounces (56 or 84 g) of the shredded pork and top with Sauerkraut Made Simple and a few slices of avocado.

Tip: If you're bringing this to the office, don't heat the sauerkraut in the microwave because it will kill the beneficial bacteria.

MEXICAN CHORIZO TACOS

These tacos are a little spicy, incredibly delicious and very nutritious. Homemade chorizo is easy to make and pairs well with the coconut crepe. The slaw makes a great side dish and only takes a few minutes to put together. A friend of mine from Colombia showed me how to make it. She ate it daily as a kid. When I first tasted it, I swore there were more ingredients in it than just lime juice, salt and some herbs. This recipe is a must try!

Makes 3 servings

INGREDIENTS

1 lb (454 g) of cooked Homemade Mexican Chorizo Sausage (page 124)

6 Coconut Crepes (page 137)

FOR THE SLAW:

½ medium-sized green cabbage, slice very thin

1 handful (about ⅓ cup [10 g]): fresh mint, minced

1 handful (about ⅓ cup [5 g]): fresh cilantro, minced

Juice from 1 lime

½ tsp salt

½ tsp red pepper flakes (optional)

INSTRUCTIONS

First combine all the slaw ingredients and if you have the time, let it sit for 1 hour before serving. To make the tacos, take one coconut crepe and add about 3 to 4 tablespoons (21 to 28 g) of the sausage, then top with 1 tablespoon (14 g) or so of the slaw. To pack for work, put the slaw in a separate container. Heat up the crepes and sausage before making the tacos and then add the slaw.

CHINESE GINGER PORK WRAP

My husband loves Chinese food but because of all the gluten in soy sauce and the bad oils used in the frying, American-restaurant Chinese food is not a healthy choice. One of his favorite childhood dishes was Moo Shi Pork, a stir-fry of pork and cabbage that you wrap in little pancakes. I decided to invent my own Asian-inspired stir-fry using lots of fresh ginger. This recipe is fast, simple and satisfies your takeout craving while providing you with lots of protein, vegetables and healthy fats.

Makes about 3 lunch servings

INGREDIENTS

1 tbsp (14 g) coconut oil

1 small onion, diced

3 stalks celery, diced

3 cloves garlic, minced

4 peeled grated parsnips (you could substitute carrots or 1 small sweet potato here)

1 tsp Chinese five-spice powder

1 tsp coriander

2 tsp fresh ginger

1 to 2 tsp red pepper flakes (to taste)

1 lb (454 g) ground pork (pasture-raised if possible)

1 cup (70 g) of diced, fresh wood ear or shiitake mushrooms

5 leaves Swiss chard, diced (Napa cabbage would be a great substitute here)

1 large handful diced cilantro, diced

2 tbsp (30 ml) wheat-free tamari or coconut aminos

1 head of iceberg lettuce

INSTRUCTIONS

In a large skillet, heat the coconut oil and onion over medium heat. Add celery, garlic, grated parsnips and spices. Cook for 5 to 10 minutes, then add the ground pork and sauté for 10 minutes. Next, add the mushrooms and Swiss chard and sauté until the Swiss chard wilts, about 5 minutes or so. Turn off the heat and add the cilantro and tamari (or coconut aminos). Wash and carefully remove lettuce leaves; serve filling in leaves. If packing for the office, heat filling separately and spoon into lettuce leaves before eating.

EFFORTLESS EGG ROLLS
WITH PICKLED VEGETABLES

Eggs and sauerkraut are a great match. If you're not used to the sourness of kraut, keep on trying it and I guarantee you'll develop a taste for it. I grew up eating sugary junk food, so believe me when I say that sauerkraut was something I had to learn to love. You can use my recipe for Sauerkraut Made Simple, but there are also some pretty tasty brands out there now so try a few different types to see which ones you prefer. This dish takes minutes to make and is packed with protein, good fats, some probiotics and great minerals from the nori. Since iodine is so important for thyroid health, it's a good idea to try to incorporate some sea vegetables like nori into your diet on a regular basis. Most Americans get iodine through fortified salt, but when you switch to sea salt on the Paleo diet and cut out processed foods, it's easy to become deficient in iodine. Try these served with the Winter Beet Salad with Orange and Fennel or the Shrimp Coconut Lemongrass Soup.

Makes 2 rolls (1 lunch serving)

INGREDIENTS

4 pastured eggs

1 scallion, diced

1 tsp butter, bacon fat or coconut oil for frying

2 toasted nori wrappers

4 tbsp (36 g) Sauerkraut Made Simple (page 183) or use strore bought, such as Wildbrine Madras Curry and Cauliflower Sauverkraut Salad

1 tbsp (2 g) fish roe for garnish (optional)

INSTRUCTIONS

Mix 2 of the eggs and half of the diced scallion in a bowl. Heat a skillet over medium heat. A square-shaped omelet pan works nicely with this dish, but is not necessary. Heat the fat in the pan then pour the egg in the pan. Cook until just set. When done, place on a sheet of nori. In the center of the egg, place 2 tablespoons (18 g) sauerkraut and lay it lengthwise. Roll the seaweed and eggs up, including the sauerkraut. Garnish with fish roe if you wish. Use toothpicks to hold wraps in place if you're traveling with them.

◀ Food Container available at LunchBots.com

LAMB TZATZIKI GYROS
IN COCONUT CREPES

I used to love gyros in my pre-gluten-free days. Of course, I had no idea what gyros were made of until I set out to make a healthy Paleo version. This recipe is a little more labor intensive, but it's completely worth every second of effort. Serve this with a Greek salad or simply with greens and a squeeze of lemon and olive oil.

Makes 12 wraps (about 4 servings)

INGREDIENTS

FOR THE MEAT:

4 strips bacon

1 onion, cut into 1" (2.5 cm) chunks

1 lb (454 g) ground lamb

1 tsp salt

½ tsp pepper

1 tbsp (3 g) dried oregano

4 cloves garlic

FOR THE SAUCE:

3 tbsp (42 g) Hassle-Free Homemade Mayonnaise (page 180)

2 tbsp (2 g) dill

1 tsp mint

1 tbsp (15 ml) lemon juice

3 tbsp (45 ml) coconut milk

3 tbsp (22 g) peeled, seeded and finely chopped cucumber

Salt and pepper to taste

Hot sauce (optional)

FOR THE WRAP:

12 Coconut Crepes (page 137)

1 tomato, sliced thin

¼ of a red onion, thin sliced

INSTRUCTIONS

Place the bacon and onion in a food processor and puree into a paste. Now add the lamb, salt, pepper, oregano and garlic into the food processor with the bacon mixture and blend until smooth. Remove and place on a baking sheet lined with parchment paper. Form a loaf about 1 ½ inches (3.8 cm) high, 5 inches wide (12.5 cm) and about 10 inches (25 cm) long. Bake at 300°F (150°C, or gas mark 2) for 30 minutes. Allow to sit for 15 minutes to cool, and then transfer to the refrigerator for 2 hours or overnight. When you're ready to eat, slice the loaf into ½-inch (1.3 cm) thin pieces and place them flat on a baking sheet lined with parchment paper. Broil on the top rack of your oven for 2 minutes or until browned and crispy.

To make the tzatziki sauce, simply combine the mayo, dill, mint, lemon juice, coconut milk, cucumber and salt and pepper in a small bowl. Add a dash of hot sauce if desired. Set aside.

To assemble the wraps: On each crepe, place 3 slices of the lamb, 2 slices of tomato, a few onion slices and about 1 teaspoon of the cucumber sauce. Make about 3 wraps per person to go along with a Greek salad for a beautiful and delicious lunch. It's a little messy but absolutely delicious! Your office mates will be drooling in the next cubicle!

CHAPTER 3

Portable, Primal Salads

Salads are quick, easy and substantial enough to carry you through the rest of your afternoon without drowsiness or hunger, but let's face it: Lettuce with some leftover chicken on top can get a little boring. Luckily, I've got some exciting new salad ideas that can keep lunch quick, dynamic and delicious.

The salads in this chapter have enough crunchy veggies, satiating protein and energy-rich fats in them to leave you feeling full yet not overstuffed. And with recipes like the Vietnamese "Bun" with Pork Teriyaki and the Winter Beet Salad with Orange and Fennel, they're as nice to look at as they are nutritious! Along the way I also hope to introduce you to some new vegetables that you've never had before, like the ones used in the Hearts of Palm, Shrimp and Avocado Salad, and the Two-Minute Steak, Egg and Endive Salad.

Let's not forget the dressing: Takeout salads are usually covered in sugary dressings made with inflammatory oils. While a squeeze of fresh lemon juice and a drizzle of extra virgin olive oil is all you really need, don't forget to check out heartier options like the Happy Valley Ranch Salad Dressing and Dreamy Creamy Herb Dressing in chapter 8.

The best thing about these salads is their portability: You can assemble most of them easily, bring them to work and enjoy their lasting flavor! I made sure to utilize lettuce, vegetables and other toppings that hold up well in your lunch sack and work well on the go. Never again will you find yourself bored or disappointed with your lunch, or even worse, simply unable to eat your salad because it didn't last en route to your destination. Are you hungry yet? Let's get chopping!

TWO-MINUTE STEAK, EGG AND ENDIVE SALAD

If you're tired of having steak with plain lettuce, try this combination! Fast and delicious, this salad is a snap to put together before work and is full of flavor. It's a simple salad to make with leftover steak using endive, a rich source of vitamin K, folate, vitamin A and the minerals manganese and potassium. There's also a good amount of parsley, which is high in vitamin C. The tarragon gives the steak and eggs a nice, slightly licorice flavor.

Makes 1 serving

INGREDIENTS

1 large or 2 small endive bulbs

½ cup (16 g) parsley, chopped fine

2 tbsp (4 g) fresh tarragon, minced

4 to 6 oz (112 to 170 g) leftover grill steak (simply seasoned with salt and pepper)

1 hard-boiled egg, sliced

FOR THE DRESSING:

1 tsp Dijon mustard

1 tbsp (15 ml) red wine vinegar

2 tbsp (30 ml) olive oil

INSTRUCTIONS

Coarsely chop the endive(s) and place in a medium-sized bowl. Add the parsley and tarragon. Top with sliced steak and hard-boiled egg. Mix all dressing ingredients together and dress right before serving.

VIETNAMESE "BUN" WITH PORK TERIYAKI

I've "Paleoized" this recipe by replacing the noodles with vegetables. The pork tenderloin in this recipe is delicious, but can easily be replaced with leftover pulled pork or some simple grilled shrimp. This salad is colorful, full of vitamins and packed with flavor. Instead of peanuts, I've used macadamia nuts for some crunch.

Makes 2 to 3 servings

INGREDIENTS

¾-1 lb (340 to 454 g) marinated pork tenderloin (double the marinade recipe for Terrific Teriyaki Jerky, page 151)

⅔ cup (30 g) arame seaweed

1 zucchini

½ daikon radish, peeled

½ English cucumber

1 carrot, peeled

3 scallions, minced

3 tbsp (3 g) cilantro

3 tbsp (6 g) mint

2 tbsp (6 g) basil

2 tbsp (30 ml) rice vinegar

½ tsp lemongrass, minced

1 tbsp (15ml) fish sauce, such as Red Boat brand

½ lime, juiced

1 tbsp (15 ml) macadamia nut oil

1 tsp sriracha (see Resources)

2 tbsp (17 g) crushed macadamia nuts

INSTRUCTIONS

Double the marinade for the Terrific Teriyaki Jerky recipe and marinate the pork tenderloin in it overnight. Dry off the pork with a paper towel and sear in a skillet until done, rotating as needed, for a total of 15 minutes or until the internal temperature reaches 145°F (63°C). When done, transfer to a cutting board and allow to rest for 5 to 10 minutes before slicing thinly (about ¼ to ½ inch [6 mm to 1.3 cm] slices). Soak the seaweed in warm water for about 15 minutes or until soft. Meanwhile, with a spiral vegetable slicer or mandoline, slice the zucchini, daikon, cucumber and carrot. Combine them in a bowl with the seaweed, scallions, cilantro, mint and basil. Mix well and set aside. To make the dressing, combine the vinegar, lemongrass, fish sauce, lime juice, oil and sriracha. Dress the salad when it's time to eat and top with macadamia nuts. If bringing to work, pack the dressing in a separate container.

PROSCIUTTO AND FIG SALAD

This sweet and savory salad is a showstopper. It's beautiful and incredibly delicious. Fresh figs can be found in the fall at most grocery stores. They taste sweet, like a mix between an apple and a pear but with a softer texture. You can get extra fancy and slice the figs in quarters: Run the knife almost down to the bottom then spread the fig open like a flower. If you don't have truffle honey for this recipe, just add regular honey and some truffle oil. Serve this salad with a nice autumn soup, like the Butternut Parsnip Soup with Leeks (page 116).

Makes 1 serving

INGREDIENTS

2 cups (110 g) baby arugula

About 12 fresh basil leaves

6 oz (170 g) sliced prosciutto, torn into thin strips

4 fresh figs

½ red onion, sliced very thin (almost shaved)

pepper and salt to taste

FOR THE DRESSING:

½ tsp truffle honey (or ½ tsp regular honey with ¼ teaspoon of truffle oil)

2 tbsp (30 ml) balsamic vinegar

1 tsp fresh lemon juice

¼ cup (60 ml) olive oil

2 tbsp (14 g) crushed toasted hazelnuts

INSTRUCTIONS

For the salad, start with the arugula then top with basil leaves. Next add the prosciutto, then the figs, quartered, and top with the onion. Sprinkle with a dash of salt and pepper. To make the dressing, combine the honey and vinegar with lemon juice and mix in the olive oil. Dress right before serving and sprinkle with hazelnuts.

SPICY SALMON AND CUCUMBER "NOODLE" SALAD

It's a hot summer day and you need something light to go. This is the salad for you. This refreshing, simple dish takes only a few minutes to put together, but it tastes phenomenally delicious. Wild salmon is protein dense, has great omega-3 fatty acids and is a rich source of niacin, calcium, phosphorus and selenium. I prefer using English cucumbers versus garden cukes in this recipe because they have less water, fewer seeds and are long enough to work well in the spiral slicer. Zucchini could be substituted for the cucumber, but it would have a firmer texture.

Makes 1 serving

INGREDIENTS

1 English cucumber

1 6-oz (170 g) can wild salmon, drained

3 tbsp (6 g) mint, minced

⅛ tsp red pepper flakes

1 tbsp (15 ml) freshly squeezed lemon juice

pepper

INSTRUCTIONS

Skin the cucumber and slice on a spiral vegetable slicer. If you don't have one of these amazing tools, you can use a mandoline on a thick setting. Place the cucumber noodles in a bowl and combine with the salmon, mint, red pepper flakes, lemon and pepper.

Although cucumbers sometimes tend to get watery after slicing, I have tested these sliced noodles on the road. If you slice them in the morning and add the lemon juice later at lunchtime, they hold up surprisingly well!

GRILLED MAHI MAHI "NIÇOISE" SALAD

Warm and filling yet light at the same time, this amazing salad is my interpretation of a Niçoise. It's perfect any time of year and has a great balance of a little starch from the potatoes and a lot of protein and good fats from the fish. Mahi mahi is a beautiful and firm white fish. To support sustainable fishing, you want to look for U.S. mahi mahi that is troll/pole caught. See the Introduction for more information on sustainable fish. Cook the fish, potatoes and string beans the night before so you can assemble and go in the morning. I could eat this every day!

Makes about 3 large servings

INGREDIENTS

1 tsp ground fennel

1 tsp ground mustard

1 tsp ground coriander

½ tsp ground cardamom

½ tsp salt

½ tsp pepper

3 tbsp (45 ml) melted coconut oil

1 lb (454 g) mahi mahi

3 small waxy potatoes, like Yukon gold or fingerlings, peeled

1 lb (454 g) thin green string beans

1 tbsp (15 ml) lemon juice

¼ tsp mustard powder

2 tsp red wine vinegar

2 tbsp (30 ml) olive oil

¼ cup (35 g) capers, rinsed

1 large tomato, diced (heirlooms are terrific, like striped German or Brandywine)

2 tbsp (4 g) minced parsley

Salt and pepper to taste

INSTRUCTIONS

Heat your grill. Combine the fennel, mustard, coriander, cardamom, salt and pepper with the melted coconut oil and make a paste. Rub on both sides of the fish and set aside. While the grill is warming up, boil the potatoes for about 20 minutes or until you can just stick a fork through them. Remove from the water with a slotted spoon and set aside. Drop the string beans into the same boiling water and cook until just tender, about 5 to 8 minutes. Remove from heat and place the beans in a large bowl.

When the grill is hot, cook the fish on both sides until done, about 10 minutes total or until the fish is cooked but not dry. Remove from heat.

To make the dressing, combine the lemon juice, mustard powder, red wine vinegar and olive oil. Slice the warm potatoes into 2-inch (5 cm) chunks and place them in the bowl with the string beans. Add the capers and tomatoes. Cube the mahi mahi into 2-inch (5 cm) chunks and add them to the bowl. Drizzle the dressing over the salad and garnish with minced parsley. Salt and pepper to taste.

Food Container available at LunchBots.com ▶

HEARTS OF PALM, SHRIMP AND AVOCADO SALAD

This refreshing salad is light but filling and has a lovely citrus flavor. It's excellent alongside jerk chicken and perfect for a hot summer afternoon (or when you want it to feel like one). Hearts of palm taste a lot like artichoke hearts (which could easily be substituted in this recipe) and are a good source of many key vitamins and minerals.

Makes 2 servings

INGREDIENTS

1 clove garlic

3 tbsp (3 g) fresh cilantro

3 tbsp (6 g) fresh basil

3 tbsp (45 ml) fresh lemon juice

3 tbsp (45 ml) fresh orange juice

½ cup (120 ml) olive oil

½ tsp salt

1 can (14 oz, or 392 g) hearts of palm, drained and sliced

2 large avocadoes, diced

¼ red onion, sliced very thin

1 large tomato, diced or 1 pint cherry tomatoes, halved

3 cups (165 g) mâche lettuce or Boston lettuce leaves, torn

8 oz (228 g) grilled wild shrimp, seasoned with salt, pepper and a little lime juice

INSTRUCTIONS

To make the dressing, combine the garlic, cilantro, basil, lemon juice, orange juice and salt in a blender. Slowly add the olive oil and blend until smooth. Set aside. In a large bowl, combine the sliced hearts of palm with the avocado, red onion, lettuce and tomato. Toss with the dressing right before serving. If bringing to the office, pack the lettuce separately from the dressed avocadoes, onion and hearts of palm. Assemble at the office. You can top with the grilled shrimp or serve it on the side if you like.

◀ Food Container available at LunchBots.com

ASIAN CHICKEN "NOODLE" BOWL

My take on a peanut noodle bowl is creamy and crunchy at the same time. It satisfies any craving for takeout—and it's much healthier! In college, I used to get vegetarian peanut noodles from an earthy little restaurant and I can still remember how comforting that meal was. This dish packs in many healthy veggies, plus a shot of iodine and other minerals from the seaweed. If you're worried about the taste of seaweed, don't fret. You won't even notice it among the crunchy strips of red peppers, long strings of cucumber, zucchini, daikon and carrot, and the heavenly gado gado sauce.

Makes 2 servings

INGREDIENTS

⅔ cup (30 g) arame seaweed

½ daikon radish

½ large carrot (choose one that is thick if using the spiral vegetable slicer)

1 small or ½ large zucchini

½ of an English cucumber, peeled

½ red bell pepper, cut into matchsticks

2 tbsp (2 g) cilantro, minced

1 tbsp (2 g) fresh basil, sliced

8 to 10 oz (228 to 280 g) roasted chicken, shredded

½ cup (120 ml) Creamy Cashew Gado Gado Sauce (page 178)

1 tsp sliced fresh red or green jalapeno pepper for garnish (optional)

INSTRUCTIONS

Soak the seaweed in warm water for about 15 minutes or until soft. Using a spiral vegetable slicer, slice the daikon, carrot, zucchini and cucumber into a bowl. Alternatively, you can grate the carrot and daikon, and thinly slice the zucchini and cucumber with a mandoline or a knife. Drain the seaweed. Add the seaweed, red pepper, cilantro and basil to the bowl of sliced veggies. Warm the gado gado sauce and chicken. Top the "noodles" with the chicken and warm gado gado sauce. If bringing to the office, pack the gado gado sauce separately and keep it at room temperature. Add the sauce right before serving. Garnish with jalapeno, if desired.

WILD TUNA, ORANGE AND PARSLEY SALAD

I originally saw this recipe in *Bon Appétit* magazine many years ago, and have made my own little tweaks over the years. This colorful and sophisticated salad raises canned tuna to another level. I'd pay big money to eat this salad at a restaurant. Now I can prepare it at home and eat it on the go! It's the kind of lunch I could eat every day because it makes me feel so good afterward. The reason I use parsley in this recipe is because it doesn't wilt when you leave the dressing on it. As far as nutrition goes, parsley provides vitamin K while the orange and red peppers are packed with vitamin C. This dish stays crunchy over time and delivers sweet and slightly salty flavors from the oranges and capers. It may seem funny to combine oranges and tuna, but once you try this I guarantee you'll want to make it again.

Makes 2 lunch servings

INGREDIENTS

2 5-oz (140 g) cans of wild tuna (I prefer the tuna packed in olive oil)

3 cloves garlic, minced

1 red pepper, diced small

¼ red onion, diced small

2 red radishes, matchsticked

4 tbsp (35 g) capers, rinsed

2 oranges, peeled, sectioned and diced

1 large bunch of flat leaf parsley, chopped

2 tbsp (30 ml) extra virgin olive oil

1 tbsp (15 ml) red wine vinegar

pepper to taste

INSTRUCTIONS

Simply combine all of the ingredients in a bowl. Makes about 1 quart (800 g) of salad. If packing for the office, you can take it as is. Just refrigerate until you're ready to have lunch.

◀ Food Container available at LunchBots.com

WINTER BEET SALAD
WITH ORANGE AND FENNEL

If you think you don't like beets, this classic recipe is a must try. You can purchase already cooked beets in the produce section of most grocery stores these days, making this dish easy to assemble quickly. I love adding a mixture of golden, red and striped beets along with blood oranges when they're in season. This salad goes great with any leftover meat you have from the night before, which makes it a perfect Paleo lunch to take to work. Just roast the beets ahead of time and the rest is easy. Grilled mahi mahi drizzled with fresh lemon juice is my favorite protein with this salad. It will power you through your afternoon and load you up with vitamins and minerals from the vegetables.

Makes 4 servings

INGREDIENTS

4 Beets

2 tsp olive oil

3 oranges (blood oranges make it even prettier!)

1 fennel bulb

¼ red onion

1 head radicchio

½ cup (16 g) parsley, chopped

⅓ cup (5 g) cilantro, chopped

1 tsp blood orange vinegar

½ lemon

½ lime

1 tbsp (15 ml) olive oil

salt and pepper to taste

INSTRUCTIONS

If using raw beets, rinse them with water and place each one on a square of tin foil. Coat them lightly with olive oil and wrap them up. Roast for about 45 minutes at 350°F (180°C, or gas mark 4) or until you can pierce them with a fork. Remove from the oven and set aside for about 10 minutes until they are cool enough to handle but still warm. Peel the beets, slice them and place in a large bowl. Next, peel the orange. If you want to be fancy, you can section it but there are some good nutrients in the white part, so I tend just to slice the orange into bite-size pieces, leaving some white. Slice the fennel bulb thinly using a knife or mandoline. Chop the radicchio and add to the bowl with the beets and orange, then add the parsley and cilantro. Drizzle the entire salad with the vinegar, lemon juice, lime juice and olive oil. Add a dash of salt and pepper. Toss the salad. It sits well before serving as the beets take up the acids in the dressing.

Food Container available at LunchBots.com ▶

CHICKEN AVOCADO BACON SALAD

Are you ready for a hearty salad, something that is satisfying, delicious and simple to make? If you want to feel energized and avoid those drowsy afternoon slumps, eat a salad packed with protein and good fats like this one. The creamy ranch dressing is the magical ingredient that blends all of the components together. All I can say is wow—you've got to try this one!

Makes 1 large serving

INGREDIENTS

4 to 6 oz (112 to 170 g) roasted chicken, diced

½ tomato, diced

1 tbsp (10 g) diced red onion

¼ cup (30 g) peeled and diced cucumber

2 cups (110 g) romaine lettuce, diced

3 strips bacon, diced

¼ to ½ avocado, diced

2 tbsp (30 ml) Happy Valley Ranch Salad Dressing (page 181)

INSTRUCTIONS

Combine all ingredients and add the dressing right before eating. Enjoy!

STEAK SALAD WITH CURRY PICKLED VEGETABLES

I could eat this incredible salad every. Single. Day. It's bursting with color and flavor, like the combination of the salty, creamy nut sauce with sour, crunchy vegetables. When you eat this salad, you feel terrific knowing that you're honoring your body with such a nutritious meal. I have to admit that I was skeptical about mixing sauerkraut with my Creamy Cashew Gado Gado Sauce, but the combination is absolutely amazing. I love this new line of pickled vegetables by Wildbrine, but you can substitute your favorite kind of sauerkraut and get similar results.

Makes 2 servings

INGREDIENTS

½ cup (120 ml) Creamy Cashew Gado Gado Sauce (page 178)

1 tbsp (14 g) coconut oil

¾ lb (340 g) steak tips or sliced grilled steak (freshly cooked or left over from dinner the night before)

¼ tsp salt

½ tsp pepper

3 cups (165 g) baby arugula, washed

1 red bell pepper, sliced thin

4" (10 cm) piece of daikon radish, peeled and sliced thin

1 carrot, peeled and grated

8 basil leaves, julienned

½ cup (70 g) curry sauerkraut (I prefer Wildbrine Madras Curry & Cauliflower Sauerkraut Salad)

INSTRUCTIONS

Make the Creamy Cashew Gado Gado Sauce and add 3 tablespoons (45 ml) coconut milk to thin the sauce and bring it to room temperature. Place the arugula, pepper, daikon, carrot and ¼ cup of the thinned gado gado sauce in a large bowl. Slice the steak into thin strips. Top the salad with the steak, then the basil. Top the whole mixture with the curry sauerkraut.

Tip: If you're taking this to work, bring the gado gado sauce and steak on the side and heat separately before adding to the salad. The other ingredients will hold up nicely mixed together in a container in your insulated bag or refrigerator.

Office-Ready Soups and Stews

Ah, my favorite way to eat! Some people like to bake; I love to make soup. There's something so peaceful and grounding about making a big pot of nutrient-dense goodness for my family. I love a warm bowl of homemade broth with slow-cooked, tender meat and hearty vegetables. I have to admit that most of my meals are consumed like this. Because I'm running between school drop-off, working out, seeing nutrition clients in my home office, attending a class, catching the runaway pigs (yeah, I'm not kidding!) and back again, soups and stews fit into my lifestyle. I start one like the Creamy Indian Goat Curry on the stove in the morning when I get back from my gym and then check on it after I walk my kids home from school.

And speaking of kids, soups and stews are an excellent way to sneak in vegetables without having to hear all the whining. Or maybe you've got a partner who is less than adventurous when it comes to vegetables. The recipes that follow can easily be modified to suit your preferences or your family's. What? Your kids don't like spicy bok choy? Mine don't either. Try the less spicy version of the Chicken, Vegetable and Avocado Soup so everyone can be happy.

As far as portability goes, few meals are easier to pack up for work than a soup or stew. All you need is a spoon and a microwave! And unlike salads, which should be made fresh, the flavor of soups and stews actually improves on the second or third day. If you want fast, try the no-cook, ready-in-under-ten-minutes, Peppery Smooth Gazpacho made in a blender. If you want exotic, the Brazilian Fish Stew will transport your taste buds to South America and the Shrimp Coconut Lemongrass Soup is a burst of Thailand without the flight. Nourishing, filling, delicious and portable, I know you'll find some amazing soup and stew recipes to love in the pages that follow.

ORANGE FENNEL CARROT SOUP

When summer is winding down and I've got a field full of carrots and fennel waiting to be used, I make this soup and everybody cheers. Even my kids! Warm and comforting, this dish is great alongside the Grilled Mahi Mahi "Niçoise" Salad. Carrots have an incredible amount of beta-carotene, which gets converted to vitamin A in the intestines and is a powerful antioxidant. I love making vegetable puree soups and drinking them like tea from a mug while I work. I bet you will, too!

Makes about 2 quarts (2 liters)

INGREDIENTS

2 tbsp (28 g) ghee

1 large leek, rinsed and diced (about 2 cups [200 g])

1 small celeriac, peeled and diced (about 1 cup [120 g])

1 fennel bulb, diced plus 2 tbsp (4 g) of the fronds, minced

1 tsp fennel seed

3 large carrots, peeled and diced (about 3 cups [360 g])

1 tsp dried thyme

4 cloves garlic

2 quarts (2 liters) No-Stress Homemade Chicken Stock (page 156)

1 orange

½ cup (120 ml) full-fat coconut milk

2 tbsp (4 g) fresh rosemary, minced

2 tbsp (4 g) fresh mint, minced

salt and pepper to taste

Balsamic vinegar and fennel fronds for garnish (optional)

INSTRUCTIONS

Warm the ghee in a large soup pot. Add the leeks, celeriac, fennel, fennel seed, carrots, thyme and garlic. Sauté until the leeks are tender, about 5 to 10 minutes. Add the chicken stock and bring to a boil. Reduce the heat and simmer, uncovered, for about ½ hour. Remove from heat. Grate ½ the orange rind (about 1 teaspoon or so) and juice the orange. Add the coconut milk, orange juice and rind, rosemary and mint to the soup and with an immersion blender puree until smooth. Add salt and pepper to taste. Garnish with a drizzle of balsamic vinegar and fennel fronds.

LEMON SPINACH & EGG RIBBON SOUP

This is a lovely blend of my two favorite soups: Italian stracciatella, a soup with parmesan cheese and breadcrumbs, and the Greek soup avgolemono, which is an egg-lemon soup containing rice or pasta. I removed the starch and cheese and combined the best of both soups to come up with this family favorite. The bonus is that my kids absolutely love it! I always have eggs, mushrooms and greens in the fridge and a freezer full of chicken stock so I can make this soup any time I like. You can add a pinch of red pepper flakes if you want a touch of heat. Try this soup with the Zucchini, Prosciutto and Basil Pinwheels (page 56).

Makes about 6 servings

INGREDIENTS

2 tsp coconut oil or ghee

1 small onion, diced small

4 cloves of garlic

2 quarts (2 liters) No-Hassel Homemade Chicken Stock (page 156)

8 shiitake mushrooms that have been diced and sautéed in butter or ghee

1 to 2 cups (140 to 280 g) shredded leftover chicken (I use what's left over from making the broth)

2 cups (60 g) diced spinach or Swiss chard, diced very small

4 pasture-raised eggs, beaten

2 lemons, juiced and one grated rind

salt and pepper to taste

3 tbsp (6 g) fresh parsley

INSTRUCTIONS

In a soup pot, sauté the onion and garlic in the coconut oil. After the onion is soft, add the chicken broth and mushrooms. Bring to a simmer. Add the chicken and spinach and cook for just a few minutes. Don't let the spinach get overcooked. Turn off the heat. Pour the beaten eggs into the soup stirring to evenly distribute the egg strands with a spoon. Add the lemon rind and lemon juice plus salt and pepper to taste. Serve and garnish with fresh parsley.

FIERY SWEET DUMPLING CHILI

This chili is a bowl full of warmth and comfort. It's a smart dish as it uses leftover meat as its base. Grass-fed beef and pork chops are great the first night if you cook them right, but as leftovers they can be tough and chewy. I decided to take the sweet dumpling squash—which is similar to acorn squash—and combine it with diced leftover beef that softens nicely in this delicious chili. You can substitute one small butternut, two acorn or three delicata. I always like to try to sneak a little seaweed into my stews; they boost the nutrition of this soup to a whole new level. The chipotle in here makes it spicy, but the coconut milk blends all the flavors into a creamy chili that is a sure winner.

Makes about 3 to 4 servings

INGREDIENTS

2 sweet dumpling squash

1 tbsp (14 g) coconut oil

2 tsp cumin

1 tsp dried thyme

1 onion, diced

4 cloves garlic, minced

¼ tsp chili powder

¼ tsp cinnamon

¼ tsp ground cloves

1 red pepper, diced

1 tbsp (8 g) chipotle chili in adobo sauce, minced

1 quart (560 g) leftover diced beef and/or pork

1 28-oz (784 g) can diced tomatoes

1 pint (470 ml) homemade stock (chicken, turkey, or beef)

⅓ cup (18 g) wakame seaweed

½ cup (120 ml) full-fat coconut milk

3 tbsp (3 g) fresh cilantro, minced

salt and pepper to taste

INSTRUCTIONS

Preheat the oven to 300°F (150°C, or gas mark 2). Peel, seed and chop the squash into 1 ½-inch (3.8 cm) pieces. Using scissors, cut seaweed into ½-inch (1.3 cm) pieces. In a Dutch oven over medium heat, warm the coconut oil and add the squash, spices, onion, garlic, red pepper and chipotle. Cook for about 5 minutes or until onions are soft. Add the meat and continue to cook for another 3 minutes. Now add the tomatoes and stock. Bring to a simmer and stir well. Add the seaweed into the simmering pot. Pop in the oven for about 2 ½ to 3 hours, checking in and stirring occasionally. Allow to cool slightly before serving. Add coconut milk as it cools. Salt and pepper to taste. Garnish with fresh cilantro.

Tip: I'm not a big fan of slow cookers but if you *must* use one in place of a Dutch oven, set it on low for about 10 to 12 hours.

CHICKEN, VEGETABLE AND AVOCADO SOUP

If you're sick of regular old boring chicken soup, try this new twist on an old classic. This comforting soup actually has two versions: The basic recipe is for the kids and the adult recipe has some additional veggies and heat. The result is a happy family, with everyone getting a hearty and satisfying meal. This soup is packed with healthy vegetables, protein and fats to nourish you all afternoon long.

Makes about 4 servings

INGREDIENTS

1 tbsp (14 g) coconut oil or ghee

1 onion, diced

3 cloves garlic, minced

1 tbsp (4 g) dried thyme

2 bay leaves

6 carrots, peeled and diced

4 stalks celery, diced

1 ½ quarts (1.5 liters) chicken broth (homemade, see page 156)

2 cups (280 g) shredded chicken meat from a roasted bird

4 tbsp (8 g) fresh parsley, minced

salt and pepper to taste

ADD-ONS FOR
THE SPICY VERSION:

4 cups (360 g) baby bok choy, diced

2 tbsp (28 g) coconut oil

1 tbsp (15 ml) sriracha (more or less depending on your taste)

2 scallions, diced

Handful of cilantro, diced

1 avocado, diced

INSTRUCTIONS

In a large pot, heat the coconut oil over medium heat and add the onion, garlic and thyme. Cook for about 5 minutes, and then add the bay leaf, carrots and celery. Cook for another 5 or so minutes then add the chicken broth and bring to a simmer. Simmer for 15 minutes. Add the chicken, parsley and salt and pepper for about 5 minutes and you're done.

To make a second version for the adults, sauté the bok choy in the coconut oil in a separate pan until wilted. Add the hot sauce, scallions and cilantro. Dish out the original soup mix for everyone, and then top off the "big people" bowls with half of the bok choy mixture. Top with ¼ to ½ avocado per dish.

SHRIMP COCONUT LEMONGRASS SOUP

This is my go-to soup when I'm feeling run down. I came up with this version of Tom Kha Gai with ingredients that can easily be found at most supermarkets. It doesn't take long to make and it has a rich, deep flavor without being overly spicy. If you like it to have more kick, simply add more sriracha.

Makes about 5 servings

INGREDIENTS

1 quart (1 liter) No-Stree Homemade Chicken Stock (page 156)

2 red peppers, sliced

1 12-oz (336 g) package of white or crimini mushrooms, sliced

2" (5 cm) piece of fresh ginger, peeled and grated

1 tbsp (15 g) red curry paste

1 tsp fresh lemongrass (you can buy it pre-chopped in the produce section of some stores)

2 tbsp (30 ml) gluten free fish sauce (like Red Boat brand)

1 tsp sriracha (see Resources)

1 ½ lb (680 g) shrimp (wild shrimp is a more sustainable choice)

1 14-oz (392 g) can full-fat coconut milk

1 lime, zest and juice

2 scallions, chopped (white and green parts)

3 tbsp (3 g) cilantro, minced

2 tbsp (4 g) fresh basil, minced

INSTRUCTIONS

Combine the chicken broth, peppers, mushrooms, ginger, curry paste, lemongrass, fish sauce and sriracha and bring to a simmer for 5 minutes. Add the shrimp, coconut milk, lime zest and juice and cook a few minutes or until the shrimp is done. Turn off the heat and add the scallions, cilantro and basil. It's that simple. The coconut milk will separate when the soup is stored in the fridge, but the whole soup comes back together when reheated.

Tip: You can easily substitute another kind of fish or shredded chicken for the shrimp in this recipe if you like.

CREAMY INDIAN GOAT CURRY

This dish will fill your house with the most amazing aroma for hours as it simmers in the oven. While it does require more time to make than my quick wraps, you will end up with a creamy, soothing and deep curry dish with tender meat and hearty vegetables and leftovers you can easily take to work and show off to your coworkers. I first made this dish with grass-fed beef, but then I tried it again with goat meat and it really blew me away. I leave the goat meat on the bone—it's easier to eat the meat off the bone later than to cut it off before cooking, and you get more of the meat while adding to the richness of the stew. Lamb and venison would also work very well in this recipe. Spend a little time prepping this dish in the beginning then relax while it bubbles away. It makes enough for the most amazing leftovers in the world.

Makes 4 to 6 servings

INGREDIENTS

3 lbs (1,362 g) of grass-fed beef for stew, or 4 ½ lbs (2,043 g) of pasture-raised goat meat

5 tbsp (70 g) of coconut oil

2 medium onions, diced

3 cloves of garlic, minced

2 tbsp (12 g) minced ginger

2 tsp coriander

1 tbsp (7 g) cumin

1 tsp turmeric

½ tsp cardamom

½-1 tsp red pepper flakes

4 cups (940 ml) homemade beef, lamb or chicken broth

1 cinnamon stick (or use ½ tsp ground cinnamon)

1 14-oz (392 g) can full-fat coconut milk

8 carrots, peeled and diced

1 lb (454 g) mushrooms, sliced in half

Salt and pepper to taste

½ cup (8 g) fresh cilantro, chopped

INSTRUCTIONS

Preheat oven to 300°F (150°C, or gas mark 2). Cut meat into 1 to 2-inch (2.5 to 5 cm) pieces. In a large Dutch oven, heat 3 tablespoons (42 g) of coconut oil and brown the meat in small batches. Remove all of the browned meat to a bowl and add the remaining coconut oil, onion, garlic, ginger, spices and cinnamon to the Dutch oven. Sauté for approximately 10 minutes, then return the meat and add broth. Bring to a simmer then cover and place in the oven for about 3 hours. Check periodically to ensure that there is enough liquid. If it looks dry, add a little water or broth to cover the meat. After 3 hours, add the coconut milk, mushrooms and carrots. Replace the cover and leave in the oven for 1 more hour. Remove from heat and remove the cinnamon stick. Add the cilantro, salt and pepper to taste. Serve.

To cool, leave on stove for about 1 hour then transfer to smaller containers (I like 2- and 3-cup [470 and 705 ml] glass storage containers which can easily go from freezer to fridge to microwave.)

Tip: I'm not a big fan of slow cookers but if you *must* use one in place of a Dutch oven, set it on low and cook for 10 to 12 hours checking on it every few hours.

PEPPERY SMOOTH GAZPACHO
(FOR PEOPLE WHO HATE GAZPACHO)

I'm normally not a fan of gazpacho. It tends to have a bitter and acidic taste. After lots of attempts to befriend this soup, I've struck gold with this recipe. I use a lot more cucumber and black pepper than most recipes, which gives the dish a fresh, light and spicy taste. It's super quick to whip up in your blender before heading out the door. All you need is a side of protein, like a beautiful piece of grilled wild salmon, to round out your meal.

Makes 4 to 6 servings

INGREDIENTS

1 28-oz (784 g) can peeled whole tomatoes (if using fresh tomatoes, use 8 large plum tomatoes and see tip)

1 cup (160 g) diced red onion

1 large garlic clove

1 small jalapeno pepper, seeded and chopped

⅓ cup (10 g) loosely packed basil leaves

2 cups (240 g) cucumber, peeled and diced (one long English cucumber)

Juice of 1 lime

2 tsp balsamic vinegar

2 tsp Worcestershire sauce (see Resources)

½ tsp salt

¾ tsp pepper

INSTRUCTIONS

Combine all ingredients in a blender and puree. Taste for salt and adjust as needed. That's it—gazpacho perfection!

Tip: To peel the tomatoes, score X's in the bottom of the tomatoes and drop in a pot of boiling water for 15 to 30 seconds, then remove to an ice bath and peel. Proceed with directions above.

BRAZILIAN FISH STEW
(*MOQUECA DE PEIXE*)

I love the combination of coconut milk, red peppers and tomatoes with the white fish. Feel free to substitute other firm fish or shellfish like mahi mahi, scallops or even lobster to take advantage of the freshest options at the market.

Makes 4 to 6 servings

INGREDIENTS

⅓ cup (80 ml) lime juice

½ tsp salt

½ tsp pepper

2 garlic cloves, minced

1 ½ lb (680 g) firm white fish cut into 1" (2.5 cm) pieces

1 ½ lb (680 g) wild caught shrimp

2 tbsp (28 g) coconut or palm oil

2 cups (320 g) chopped yellow onion

2 cups (300 g) chopped red pepper

1 cup (100 g) minced green onions

5 garlic cloves, minced

2 bay leaves

2 cups (360 g) diced tomato

1 tbsp (16 g) tomato paste

½ cup (8 g) fresh cilantro, chopped

2 cups (470 ml) fish or seafood stock

1 cup (235 ml) chicken stock

1 14-oz (392 g) can full-fat coconut milk

¼ tsp red pepper flakes

INSTRUCTIONS

Combine the first 6 ingredients in a large bowl. Set aside. Add the coconut oil or palm oil to a large soup pot and add the onion. Cook until soft. Add the pepper, green onions, garlic and bay leaf. Sauté for approximately 10 minutes or until vegetables are softened. Add tomatoes and tomato paste and cook for another 5 minutes. Add the chicken and fish stock along with the cilantro and simmer for about 10 to 15 minutes. Finally, add the coconut milk, red pepper and fish. Cook for about 3 minutes. Adjust for salt and pepper and serve.

BUTTERNUT PARSNIP SOUP
WITH LEEKS

This is the kind of soup that warms you to your bones. A little bit spicy and bursting with fall flavors, it's perfect to bring to work along with your favorite protein. I like to pair it with leftover, slow-roasted lamb. It's simple and easy to make, even on a busy weeknight. Roasting the vegetables before you boil them brings out more of their sweetness. It's even good enough to serve at your Thanksgiving table—I did!

Makes about 4 servings

INGREDIENTS

1 butternut squash, peeled and diced

6 parsnips, peeled and sliced

1 leek, sliced

1 tsp cumin

1 tsp coriander

¼ tsp cinnamon

¼ tsp freshly grated ginger

½ tsp salt

½ tsp pepper

½ tsp red pepper flakes (more or less, depending on how hot you like it)

2 tbsp (30 ml) coconut oil, melted

2 quarts (2 liters) No-Hassel Homemade Chicken Stock (page 156)

2 cups (470 ml) full-fat coconut milk

½ orange, juiced

2 tbsp (2 g) cilantro, for garnish

INSTRUCTIONS

Preheat oven to 350°F (180°C, or gas mark 4). Line a baking sheet with parchment paper. In a large bowl, combine the squash, parsnips, leeks, spices and melted coconut oil. Lay out the mixture on the baking sheet and roast for 45 minutes. Remove from the oven and transfer into a large soup pot. Add the chicken stock to the squash mixture. Bring to a boil and then reduce the heat and let simmer for approximately 10 minutes. Puree the soup with a hand blender or in a food processor. When smooth, add the coconut milk and orange juice. Adjust salt and pepper to your tastes. Ladle into bowls and garnish with fresh cilantro.

CHAPTER 5

Busy Morning Breakfasts

There are so many amazing choices for breakfast on the Paleo diet. I'm always surprised when someone asks me what I eat for breakfast since I "can't" have wheat. Once you eliminate processed cereals, toast and other bready products, the options for real, delicious food begin to present themselves.

Of course eggs are usually on the top of most Paleo eaters' list. They're fast to cook and full of nutrients. Make yourself a batch of the Bacon, Lemon and Greens Egg Muffins or the lovely Crabby Morning Egg Muffins and the next morning you can shower and run out the door with a portable breakfast in hand. Feel like starting your day with a speedy breakfast smoothie but don't want to drink a whole banana or load it up with sweeteners? I got your back! My smoothie recipes are delicious and their sweetness comes from herbs, spices, berries and melon instead of honey and maple syrup. You'll be amazed at how delicious and refreshing the Melon and Ginger Morning Smoothie is with its hint of cardamom spice. A boring berry smoothie gets a flavor boost in the Blueberry Cinnamon Coconut Smoothie and the Strawberry Watermelon Mint Smoothie is the perfect way to wake up to the world.

There are a lot of enticing sausage recipes in this section, too. I love to make my own sausages from meat raised here on my farm. You don't need a fancy sausage maker and casings to make sausages—here you will learn everything you need to know to make gourmet sausages like the Cherry Tarragon Breakfast Sausages right at home. Your kids will love the Sweet Apple Spice Breakfast Sausages and you'll be glad knowing you sent them off to school with a full belly, ready to learn. If you like a little spice in the morning, you'll love the Homemade Mexican Chorizo Sausage or even my Tortilla Española with Chorizo. So many options!

Leave those instant waffles and sugary flakes behind and enjoy starting your day with fresh whole eggs, healthy smoothies and sausages with ingredients you can pronounce. You'll feel satisfied, happy and alert all morning—ready to take on anything that comes your way. Bring it on!

GINGER AND SPICE
BREAKFAST SAUSAGES

These sausages are my go-to breakfast whenever I have some ground pork or goat meat in the fridge. They've got just a hint of heat, lots of herbs and spices. Making your own breakfast sausages may seem daunting if you've never done it before, but it's super easy and so much healthier for you than what you find at the store. I don't use a meat grinder or sausage casings; I simply use my hands to form small patties and fry them like they're little burgers. Try these with a ruby red grapefruit or a few slices of cantaloupe for a perfect start to your day.

Makes approximately 20 (3-inch [7.5 cm]) patties

INGREDIENTS

2 tbsp (28 g) coconut oil

2 lbs (908 g) ground pork

2 tsp salt

2 tsp pepper

2 tsp dried sage

2 tsp thyme

2 tsp oregano

1 tbsp (6 g) freshly ground fennel seeds

1 tbsp (8 g) freshly grated ginger

⅛ tsp freshly ground cloves

⅛ tsp nutmeg

⅛ tsp cayenne pepper

INSTRUCTIONS

Heat coconut oil over medium heat in a large skillet. Place all ingredients in a bowl and mix well with your hands until fully incorporated. Form into small patties about ½-inch (1.3 cm) thick and 3 inches (7.5 cm) in diameter. Place in the pan and fry in batches. Flip after about 7 to 10 minutes and fry for another 5 minutes on the other side. Serve. Any leftovers can be stored in the fridge and reheated in a toaster oven at 350°F (180°C, or gas mark 4) for approx 5 to 10 minutes for a quick weekday breakfast.

CHERRY TARRAGON
BREAKFAST SAUSAGES

This recipe is a winner. The combination of the sweet cherries with the aromatic, slightly licorice taste of the tarragon will infuse your morning with warmth. If you have ground venison, wild boar or other game meat, try substituting it for the pork. Leaner meats would benefit from a few ounces of pureed bacon to add some fat and moisture. Forget the pancakes, waffles, or cereal: A handful of these sausages are all you need to keep you full all morning long. Consider making mini versions of these as appetizers for parties.

Makes about 14 sausages

INGREDIENTS

½ cup (75 g) dried cherries

2 tbsp (20 g) diced onion

2 tbsp (4 g) fresh parsley, minced

2 tbsp (4 g) fresh tarragon, minced

1 tsp salt

1 tsp pepper

1 lb (454 g) ground pork (pasture-raised if possible)

2 tbsp (28 g) coconut oil for frying

INSTRUCTIONS

Place the cherries in a bowl of hot water for about 10 minutes to slightly reconstitute them. Combine the onion, parsley, tarragon, salt and pepper in a medium-sized bowl and mix well. Add the cherries when soft, and then add the ground pork. Mix all ingredients well. Form small patties (I usually can fit them in the palm of my hand) and place on a plate. Heat a skillet to medium heat and add some of the coconut oil. Place about 5 to 7 of the patties in the pan. Fry the patties until brown, about 5 minutes. Flip and flatten with the back of your spatula. Cook another 5 minutes or until brown. Test one sausage to make sure the center is completely cooked. Enjoy!

CURRIED **GREEN EGGS AND HAM**

Here's a terrific way to get some veggies into your morning in a delicious, easy way. I like to make the first half of these for my kids with no curry or red pepper, then add half of the curry and red pepper in for the grown-ups. This way, we all win! I got the idea for these from my Ecuadorian farm interns who call them tortillas. I added the curry and a hint of heat to make them my own. Follow this recipe with the full amount of spices if you're cooking for adults.

Makes about 12 (3-inch [7.5 cm]) pancakes

INGREDIENTS

1 tsp coconut oil

½ onion, diced finely

8 oz (228 g) spinach, diced small

1 cup (150 g) of ham, cubed into
½" (1.3 cm) pieces

4 eggs

1 tbsp (8 g) potato starch

¼ cup (4 g) minced fresh cilantro

2 tsp curry powder

Pinch of red pepper flakes, about
⅛ tsp

½ tsp salt

½ tsp pepper

INSTRUCTIONS

In a medium-sized skillet, warm the coconut oil. Add the onion and sauté for 5 minutes or until the onion is soft. Add the diced spinach and sauté for about 3 minutes, just until it wilts. Remove from heat and place the spinach mixture into a large bowl. In a hot pan, sauté the ham chunks until lightly browned, about 5 minutes. Remove from heat, add to the spinach mixture and set aside. Separate 4 of the eggs, adding the yolks to the spinach mixture and placing the whites in a separate bowl. Whisk the 3 whites until fluffy. Gently fold in the whites to the spinach mixture, also adding in the potato starch, cilantro, curry, red pepper flakes, salt and pepper. Be careful not to over mix and deflate the fluffy whites. Once the mixture is incorporated, you're ready to start frying them up. Warm the skillet over medium heat and melt 1 teaspoon of coconut oil. Drop about ¼ cup (56 g) of the mixture for each pancake. When the edges look cooked and the bottom is light brown, flip and continue cooking on the other side until done.

HOMEMADE MEXICAN CHORIZO SAUSAGE

This is an amazing alternative to taco filling and it's not too hot for the little ones, especially if you remove the cayenne pepper. I was visiting my dad in Arizona, where you can buy fresh chorizo at the market if you don't mind it extra salty and filled with lots of strange ingredients that are hard to pronounce. He suggested trying to make this dish together so we did—and we both absolutely loved it! This recipe is incredibly versatile: It's excellent with a fried egg, stuffed into peppers, or served in my Mexican Chorizo Tacos on page 76.

Makes about 2 quarts (940 g)

INGREDIENTS

6 dried New Mexico chili peppers

6 cloves garlic, chopped

3 tbsp (21 g) smoked paprika

1 tbsp (3 g) oregano

1 tsp cumin

½ tsp cloves

½ tsp coriander

½ tsp cayenne pepper

1 tsp salt

1 tsp pepper

2 lb (908 g) ground pork

Juice of 1 lime

4 tbsp (4 g) minced cilantro

INSTRUCTIONS

Warm a skillet and toast the chili peppers over high heat for 2 minutes a side. Remove from heat and, with scissors, clip off and discard the tops. Cut the chilies into ½-inch (1.3 cm) strips, saving the seeds. Cover with ½ cup hot water and set aside for 10 minutes while they soften. In a food processor, place the garlic, paprika, oregano, cumin, cloves, coriander, cayenne and salt and pepper. Add the softened chilies and their water. Puree into a paste. Place the pork in a large bowl and combine the puree in with your hands, being careful not to overmix. You can form the meat into patties or fry it loosely. When fully cooked, squeeze the lime juice over the sausage and sprinkle with cilantro. Serve with a fried egg or in the Mexican Chorizo Tacos.

CRABBY MORNING EGG MUFFINS

Here's a wonderful version of egg muffins that makes a terrific breakfast, brunch or lunch. These "muffins" are excellent with a big arugula salad on the side. The basil brings a welcome freshness to these savory protein-packed bites. You can even make them as mini muffins and serve them as a warm appetizer at a party.

Makes 12 regular-sized muffins

INGREDIENTS

1 tbsp (14 g) coconut oil or bacon fat to grease the muffin tins

8 eggs

1 tbsp (8 g) coconut flour

7 spears steamed asparagus, chopped into ½" (1.3 cm) pieces

2 scallions, minced

8 sundried tomatoes, minced

2 tbsp (4 g) fresh basil, minced

Freshly ground pepper

1 6.5-oz (182 g) can of all natural crabmeat

½ cup (120 ml) half-and-half or coconut milk

INSTRUCTIONS

Preheat the oven to 350°F (180°C, or gas mark 4) and grease a regular-sized muffin tin with about 1 tablespoon (14 g) coconut oil or bacon fat. In a large bowl, combine all of the ingredients and mix well. Pour into the muffin tins and bake for 15 to 18 minutes or until done.

SWEET POTATO APPLE-CINNAMON
PANCAKES

This recipe is super easy, fast and delicious. It's a big hit for kids and it's an easy breakfast to take on the go. The apple is sweet enough that it doesn't need any maple syrup or honey drizzled on top. The inside of these is sort of like soft and gooey apple pie filling. We like to have these on cold fall mornings when New England apples are in season and our wood stove is cranking in the kitchen. These delicious cakes can be served alongside homemade sausages for protein. Make a double batch; they're great reheated!

Make 4 large pancakes

INGREDIENTS

1 cup (225 g) cold, leftover mashed
sweet potatoes

1 apple (I like Gala apples), peeled
and grated

1 egg

1 tsp cinnamon

5 tbsp (40 g) potato starch

¼ tsp salt

Coconut oil or bacon fat for frying

INSTRUCTIONS

Combine all ingredients and 4 cakes. Fry in coconut oil or bacon fat in a skillet over medium heat until a brown crust is formed (about 5 minutes). Flip and flatten a bit with the back of your spatula. Cook for another 3 to 5 minutes and remove from heat. Enjoy!

HERBED OMELET
WITH TRUFFLE BUTTER

I'm just crazy about truffles. My husband and I were lucky enough to travel to Italy a few years ago during truffle season (in the fall) and brought back fresh truffles, truffle oil and truffle-infused honey for our friends. This simple omelet is made ultra-decadent with the addition of truffle butter and it takes hardly any time to make. Truffle butter can be found at most gourmet shops or in the specialty section of natural food stores like Whole Foods. If you can't find the butter, get some truffle oil and use it the same way. Yes, this ingredient is expensive but a little goes a long way. If you're in a huge rush, just cook some scrambled eggs and drizzle truffle oil on them. Because it tastes so rich, you'll never miss the toast.

Makes 1 serving

INGREDIENTS

3 whole eggs

1 tbsp (1 g) fresh chives, minced

1 tbsp (2 g) fresh parsley, minced

1 tbsp (15 ml) coconut milk

1 tsp butter or ghee for frying

1 tsp truffle butter (if you're not eating dairy, substitute truffle oil)

INSTRUCTIONS

Heat a skillet to medium heat. In a bowl, add the eggs, herbs and coconut milk and whisk together. Melt the butter in the pan and add the egg mixture. Allow to set slightly (about 1 minute), then add the truffle butter in small sections along the middle strip of the omelet. Fold both sides in and once the egg is cooked, remove from heat and serve. Enjoy!

LAMB SAUSAGE
WITH PEPPERS AND HERBS

You haven't had a truly great morning until you've tried these lamb sausages. Ground lamb is very popular in my house because it's versatile and makes, among other things, delicious sausages and meatballs. This dish is wonderful for breakfast but it would also make a great lunch or dinner, as it's not spiced specifically with breakfast in mind. It's bursting with herb and pepper flavor with just a tiny kick from the cayenne. It goes really well with Roasted Delicata Squash, page 176.

Makes 3 servings

INGREDIENTS

1 lb (454 g) ground lamb

1 tsp fennel seeds, ground

1 tsp dried sage

½ tsp dried rosemary, ground

¼ tsp cayenne pepper

½ tsp pepper

½ tsp salt

1 tsp onion powder

1 tsp granulated garlic

INSTRUCTIONS

Mix all ingredients well and form small sausage patties or logs. Sauté on all sides until completely cooked through, about 20 minutes total.

PEAR, SAGE AND FENNEL MORNING SAUSAGES

These sausages are perfect with a little fresh fruit for a fall breakfast. Larger sausage patties are great with an arugula salad for lunch!

Makes about 14 sausages

INGREDIENTS

1 pear, diced into ¼" (6 mm) pieces (or you can grate it)

3 scallions, minced

1 tsp freshly ground fennel seeds

1 tsp ground sage

1 tsp pepper

1 tsp salt

1 lb (454 g) ground pork

1 to 2 tbsp (15 to 30 ml) coconut oil for frying

INSTRUCTIONS

In a medium bowl, combine all ingredients except the pork and coconut oil and mix well. Then, add the pork and combine. Form patties, about the size of your palm, and put on a plate. In a skillet over medium heat, warm the coconut oil. Place about 5 to 7 (depending on the size) of the patties in a pan and fry for about 5 minutes or until light brown. Flip and flatten a bit with the back of your spatula. Cook for another 5 minutes or until fully cooked through. These store for up to 6 days in the refrigerator, but they won't last that long!

SWEET APPLE SPICE BREAKFAST SAUSAGES

I make extra and reheat them on busier days. A few of these sausages and a handful of fresh berries for breakfast will keep me full for a long time. They also make a terrific quick snack between meals.

Makes about 18 (2-inch [5 cm] round) sausage patties

INGREDIENTS

1 apple, peeled and grated

1 lb (454 g) ground pork

1 tbsp (15 ml) maple syrup

1 tsp fresh ginger, minced

½ tsp salt

½ tsp pepper

1 tsp bacon fat or coconut oil for frying

INSTRUCTIONS

Combine all of the ingredients and form small, palm-sized sausages. Heat a skillet over medium heat and add 1 teaspoon of bacon fat or coconut oil. Place enough sausages in the pan to fill it without overcrowding and cook until light brown on the bottom. Flip the sausages, flatten them slightly with the back of your spatula and continue cooking until done.

GINGER SCALLION
SWEET POTATO CAKES

When people are trying to reduce their sugar intake and are having trouble with cravings, eating foods with sweet spices can help. These pancakes taste very sweet from the ginger, but have no maple syrup or honey in them at all. They're packed with vitamin A and also contain lots of vitamin C and manganese. They're great for replenishing after a highly glycogen-dependent workout. I bring them to the gym with me and eat them cold. If you're having a craving for pancakes or waffles, give this recipe a try. You'll be pumped full of nutrition to start your day on the right foot. Serve these with a side of bacon or the Lamb Sausage with Peppers and Herbs (page 131).

Makes about 6 (4-inch [10 cm]) pancakes

INGREDIENTS

2 cups (450 g) leftover mashed sweet potatoes

2 eggs

3 scallions, sliced thin

1 tbsp (6 g) minced fresh ginger

3 tbsp (6 g) fresh basil, minced

⅓ cup (42 g) potato starch

½ tsp salt

½ tsp pepper

2 tsp bacon fat or coconut oil for frying

INSTRUCTIONS

Combine all ingredients in a bowl. Warm a skillet over medium heat. Drop large spoonfuls of the batter onto the skillet to make thick 4-inch (10 cm) pancakes. Flip when the bottom is lightly browned and continue cooking until the other side is light brown. Serve with a side of bacon.

TORTILLA ESPAÑOLA
WITH CHORIZO

Each town in Spain serve a slightly different version of this classic staple. On our farm we host international agriculture students from Ecuador and Peru who also eat this regularly. I've put my own twist on Tortilla Española by adding spicy chorizo sausage. I use ghee instead of olive oil because it's more stable for frying the potatoes. This is an excellent meal for any time of the day and it keeps well in the fridge for a few days to give you more lunch options at work. Add your own twist with jalapenos, or cayenne pepper to spice it up (or use kielbasa if you'd like it less spicy).

Makes about 4 servings

INGREDIENTS

¼ cup (56 g) ghee

2 medium-sized Yukon gold potatoes, peeled and sliced to ⅛" (3 mm)

1 small onion, diced

5 cloves garlic

1 red pepper, diced

1 ½ cups (165 g) homemade (page 124) or store-bought chorizo, diced

1 tsp dried thyme

2 cups (110 g) loosely packed arugula, chopped

10 eggs

½ cup (120 ml) coconut milk or heavy cream

Generous amount of pepper (I use about 1 ½ tsp)

FOR THE SAUCE:

½ tsp smoked paprika

½ tsp cumin

1 clove garlic, minced

⅓ cup (75 g) homemade mayo

1 tbsp (15 ml) lemon juice

2 tbsp (2 g) minced cilantro

INSTRUCTIONS

In a large skillet, heat the ghee to medium high. Fry the potatoes in batches. (It takes me two batches to cook the potatoes, but will depend on the size of your skillet). You want them light brown but not crispy. Flip the potatoes when the first side is brown and continue cooking until the second side is brown. Remove to a plate. When you are done cooking the potatoes, drain off most of the ghee and add the onion, garlic, red pepper, sausage and pepper with the thyme. Sauté until the onion is soft. Remove the onion mixture to a small bowl. Now, add the potato back to the pan. I like to place them in a circular pattern, with the pieces slightly overlapping each other. Now top with the onion mixture and add the arugula. Crack the eggs in a bowl and mix with the coconut milk. Add the eggs and coconut milk to the pan. Put the skillet under a broiler on high for about 5 to 10 minutes or until the eggs are set but not burnt. To serve, flip so the potato side is on top. You can do this by flipping the entire contents of the skillet onto a plate, or by cutting individual slices out of the skillet and serving bottom side up (slightly easier the second way).

To make the sauce, combine all the ingredients and serve with tortilla slices. A fresh arugula salad dressed with blood orange vinegar and a little olive oil also goes great with this dish.

COCONUT CREPES
WITH WARM SPICED APPLES

I must have tried about ten different combinations of grain-free flours before I settled on this perfect ratio of coconut flour to tapioca starch. This is a basic Paleo crepe recipe that you can top with the warm apple cinnamon topping. They are also perfect for filling with meat and veggies for a Paleo wrap. In our house, we have these in addition to homemade sausages for a complete, nutrient-dense breakfast. To make coconut pancakes, follow the modifications noted at the bottom.

Makes about 15 (4-inch [10 cm]) crepes

INGREDIENTS

⅔ cup (86 g) tapioca starch (sometimes called tapioca flour)

⅓ cup (40 g) coconut flour

¼ tsp baking soda

½ tsp salt

2 eggs

1 ½ cups (355 ml) coconut milk, canned

4 tbsp (56 ml) coconut oil (1 tbsp [14 g] melted for the pancakes and 3 tbsp [42 g] for frying)

½ cup (120 ml) water

SPICED APPLES:

3 apples, peeled and chopped into 1-inch (2.5 cm) pieces

⅓ stick butter

1 tsp cinnamon

½ tsp nutmeg

INSTRUCTIONS

In a large bowl, combine the tapioca starch, coconut flour, baking soda and salt. Mix well and break up any lumps in the coconut flour. In another bowl, combine the wet ingredients using only 1 tablespoon (14 g) of the coconut oil. Mix well. Combine the two bowls. In a skillet over medium heat, melt 1 tablespoon (14 g) of coconut oil. Place about 4 tablespoons (60 ml) of the batter on the skillet. Once the bottom is lightly browned (about 3 minutes, depending on how hot the skillet is), flip the crepe and allow to cook for about 1 more minute. Top with a small pad of butter or serve with warm spiced apples and homemade sausages. Feel free to double this recipe and make enough for tomorrow morning. They store very well in the refrigerator.

To make pancakes: Use 1 cup (235 ml) coconut milk, ⅓ cup (80 ml) water and add ½ cup (120 ml) pure maple syrup (optional) and 1 teaspoon cinnamon.

To make Spiced Apples: Saute the apples, cinnamon and nutmeg in the butter for about 8-10 minutes or until soft.

BACON, LEMON AND GREENS
EGG MUFFINS

My trainer once told me, "The egg muffin is the secret weapon of any successful Paleo person." I agree! Once you've made a batch of these and see how portable and easy they are to make, you'll be making them weekly. I've tried all kinds of combinations including sausage and roasted red peppers, artichoke hearts and prosciutto, and many more. I really love the lemon flavor in these because it's a little wake-up call for your mouth. The small amount of coconut flour and coconut milk help them stay very moist. Mini egg muffins are also fun for kids, especially when they can add their favorite ingredients to them. All-natural hot dogs in the center are a big hit at our house!

Makes 12 regular-sized muffins

INGREDIENTS

2 tbsp (30 ml) of fat from the bacon (or coconut oil)

½ onion, minced

4 leaves of Swiss chard (or spinach or kale), diced pretty small

8 eggs

¼ cup (60 ml) coconut milk

2 tbsp (16 g) of coconut flour

1 lemon, grated rind and juice

5 slices of bacon, diced

½ tsp pepper

⅛ tsp cayenne pepper (or more to taste)

INSTRUCTIONS

Preheat the oven to 350°F (180°C, or gas mark 4) and grease a muffin tin with about 1 tablespoon (15 ml) of coconut oil or bacon fat. In a skillet over medium heat, warm the rest of the bacon fat or coconut oil. Sauté the onion until soft, then add the Swiss chard and cook until just wilted, about 2 minutes. Remove from heat. In a large bowl, mix the eggs, coconut milk and coconut flour. Add the rest of the ingredients to the bowl and mix. Pour egg batter into the muffin tin. Bake for 15 to 18 minutes or until the centers look set. Remove from the oven and cool. Store in the refrigerator.

POACHED EGG WITH **TUSCAN BREAKFAST HASH**

This combination is really amazing: It's sweet tasting from the sundried tomatoes and sweet potatoes and rich from the pork and herbs. Fresh basil brightens it up and gives it a zing. It's a substantial breakfast that will power you through the morning straight through to lunch. I like making a double batch and reheating it as needed through the week for breakfast. You can poach the egg at home the traditional way, but I also offer a way to enjoy a warm, runny egg over some incredible hash right at your office. This classic dish works well for breakfast or for lunch!

Makes about 1 ½ quarts (680 g)

INGREDIENTS

1 tbsp (15 ml) bacon fat

1 onion, diced

2 cloves garlic, minced

1 Japanese sweet potato (or regular sweet potato), roasted, peeled and diced

1 tsp ground fennel seeds

1 tsp dried rosemary

1 tsp dried thyme

1 lb (454 g) pastured pork or lamb

3 tbsp (21 g) sundried tomatoes, minced

3 tbsp (6 g) fresh basil, sliced

1 egg

INSTRUCTIONS

In a large skillet, melt the bacon fat. Add the onion and sauté for about 3 minutes. Add the garlic, sweet potato, fennel seeds and dried herbs and sauté for 5 minutes. Add the ground meat and cook until done, about 7 minutes. Add the sundried tomatoes for another 3 minutes and incorporate well. Remove from heat and add the fresh basil.

To make the poached egg at your office, all you need is a microwave-safe bowl, some water and an egg. A glass dish, like Pyrex, works well for this. Crack the egg into the water and pierce the yolk once with a fork. Microwave on high for approximately 90 seconds. All microwaves are different, so adjust according to how powerful yours is. With a slotted spoon, remove the egg and serve over the warm hash.

BUBBLE AND SQUEAK
FRIED POTATO CAKES

The idea for this one comes from a traditional Irish recipe that takes leftover colcannon (mashed potatoes with boiled vegetables) from Sunday dinner and fries them up to be eaten with a fried egg for lunch or dinner. The strange name is said to be from the bubbling and squeaking in the skillet of witches and ghosts trying to escape from the heat. Not surprisingly, it is traditionally served on Halloween. In Scotland, this is called Rumbledethumps. Feel free to substitute green cabbage, spinach or Swiss chard for the kale and try using leeks instead of the onion. Serve with a fried egg on top, or with my favorite addition, smoked trout topped with crème fraîche.

Makes 20 cakes

INGREDIENTS

3 tbsp (42 g) coconut oil for frying

3 lb (1,362 g) Yukon gold potatoes (about 7 medium-sized potatoes)

1 onion, diced

6 cloves garlic, minced

1 bunch of kale, finely chopped

1 cup (235 ml) of coconut milk or cream

6 slices cooked bacon, cut into small pieces

2 eggs

1 cup (120 g) potato starch (also called potato flour)

1 tsp salt

1 tsp pepper

OPTIONAL ADDITIONS:

1 8-oz (228 g) pkg smoked trout (I like Ducktrap brand)

crème fraîche

INSTRUCTIONS

Peel the potatoes and cut them into 2-inch (5 cm) chunks. Boil until tender, about 15 minutes. Drain and allow to cool. Meanwhile, sauté the onion in 1 tablespoon (14 g) of coconut oil or some leftover bacon grease for approximately 5 minutes or until soft. Add the garlic and kale and continue cooking for another 5 to 10 minutes or until the kale is wilted and cooked through. Remove from heat. Place the cooled potatoes in a large bowl and mash with the coconut milk. They will be a bit drier and less creamy than traditional mashed potatoes but the texture should be slightly chunky. Add the kale mixture, bacon, eggs, potato starch, salt and pepper and mix well. Warm 1 teaspoon of the coconut oil in a skillet over medium heat. With your hands, form small patties about the size of a small hamburger and fry in the skillet, about 4 at a time. After about 5 minutes, when there is a nice brown crust on the bottom of the cake, flip and flatten slightly with the back of your spatula. Fry for another 5 minutes then remove to a plate. Repeat until all the cakes are cooked. Top with a 2- to 3-ounce (56 to 84 g) portion of smoked trout and 1 teaspoon of crème fraîche. A sunny-side up egg is also very nice as an alternative to the trout and crème fraîche.

Trio of Smoothies

If you're in a rush but you want a blast of good nutrition, you can't go wrong with a smoothie. All you need is a blender to make one of these three satisfying flavor combinations on a busy morning. I don't like to start my morning with a huge blast of sugar, so I omit the maple syrup and bananas from my smoothies and opt for more subtle flavors. For protein, you can add a raw pastured egg, or pair your smoothie of choice with cooked eggs or breakfast sausages. The longer you're on the Paleo diet, the sweeter simple smoothies like these will taste to you.

MELON AND GINGER MORNING SMOOTHIE

When melons are in season, they often become overripe and watery before I can enjoy them. When this happens, I chop them up and freeze them in 1-cup (235 ml) portions so that I can use them in smoothies on another day. This subtle smoothie doesn't hit you with a strong, sweet taste but rather a more subtle and delightful flavor from the ginger, cardamom and cinnamon.

Makes 1 serving

INGREDIENTS

½ **14-oz (392 g) can coconut milk**

1 cup (235 ml) water

5 ice cubes

1 cup (140 g) chopped ripe muskmelon or cantaloupe

½ tsp cardamom

½ tsp ginger

½ tsp cinnamon

⅛ tsp vanilla extract

1 raw egg (optional)

INSTRUCTIONS

Combine all in a blender or in a tall quart (liter) container with an immersion blender. (I use the second method because it's a little easier to clean up.) Pour and enjoy.

BLUEBERRY CINNAMON COCONUT SMOOTHIE

This is a warm and bright way to start your day. I suggest this to my clients who are used to drinking smoothies in the morning but are sick of plain coconut milk and water.

Makes 1 serving

INGREDIENTS

1 cup (155 g) frozen blueberries

½ 14-oz (392 g) full-fat coconut milk (mix the contents of the can if separation has occurred)

1 tsp cinnamon

1 cup (235 ml) water

Juice of ½ a lime

1 raw egg (optional)

INSTRUCTIONS

Blend all of the ingredients until smooth. That's it!

STRAWBERRY WATERMELON MINT SMOOTHIE

This bright pink smoothie is really refreshing and smooth. It's perfect for a hot summer day or after a difficult workout.

Makes 1 serving

INGREDIENTS

1 cup (255 g) frozen strawberries

1 ½ cups (225 g) diced watermelon

½ 14-oz (392 g) full-fat coconut milk

10 mint leaves

Juice of ½ lime

1 raw egg (optional)

INSTRUCTIONS

Blend all ingredients together in a blender. Enjoy!

CHAPTER 6

Entry-Level Essentials

Let me teach you the basics, like how to make Lemon Pepper Roasted Chicken, Pulled Pork with Orange and Herbs and No-Stress Homemade Chicken Stock. Don't worry—you don't need a cooking school degree to make these recipes! Here you'll find basic recipes to help you keep your busy lifestyle. You no longer have to buy expensive, Paleo-approved treats to eat on the go. My recipe for Terrific Teriyaki Jerky will save you money and add a new and satisfying snack to your regular lineup. If you want to enjoy the portability of a sandwich, branch out beyond lettuce and wrap your protein in my Sweet Potato Crepes with Chives or my Sundried Tomato Rosemary Biscuits. Both are easy to make and take on the road.

PULLED PORK
WITH ORANGE AND HERBS

I used to think pulled pork was something you needed a lot of skill to make until someone told me that you just throw a hunk of pork in a pot and let it cook for a few hours. Well, I figured I could handle that. I looked up a few recipes and then developed my own version that features a juicy, slightly citrusy flavor and just a touch of heat. There's no need to smother this pulled pork in sugary barbecue sauce—it's got plenty of flavor to hold its own! If you like this one, you may also want to try my recipe for Pulled Pork Wrap with Sauerkraut and Avocado on page 75. Serve this warm, tender meat over a bed of greens for a delicious Paleo lunch or dinner.

Makes about 1 ½ quarts (680 g) of pulled pork

INGREDIENTS

3 lbs (1,362 g) pork shoulder

2 tsp cumin

Rind from 1 orange

1 tsp each dried rosemary, thyme and fennel

1 tsp garlic powder

1 tsp onion powder

½ tsp chipotle chili powder

½ tsp salt

½ tsp pepper

2 tbsp (30 ml) bacon fat

½ cup (120 ml) chicken broth

INSTRUCTIONS

To make the pulled pork, combine the cumin, orange, herbs, garlic, onion powder, chili powder, salt and pepper. Rub all over the pork. Allow to marinate for 2 to 6 hours. In a Dutch oven, heat the bacon fat. Sear the pork on all sides. Add the chicken broth. Cover the pot and place in a 250°F (120°C, or gas mark ½) oven for 3 to 4 hours. When it's done cooking, remove the pork from the pot and shred it using two forks. Place in a bowl. Add a little of the cooking liquid to moisten the meat. It's ready to enjoy!

LEMON PEPPER **ROASTED CHICKEN**

Many people I sell chickens to have no idea what to do with a whole chicken. I prefer roasting an entire chicken rather than buying boneless, skinless chicken breasts because I can use the rest of that chicken for making No-Stress Homemade Chicken Stock (page 156). The best place to buy your chickens is from a farmer and the most sustainable form of chicken to purchase is one that has already served the purpose of laying eggs. Old egg layers, however, are not the most tender and moist birds to roast. I save those chickens for direct entry into the stockpot. I typically roast chicken about 2 to 3 times a month.

Makes 3 to 4 servings

INGREDIENTS

1 3- to 4-lb (1,362 to 1,816 g) roasting chicken

2 tbsp (28 g) coconut oil, bacon fat, lard or duck fat, melted

2 tsp salt

1 tbsp (5 g) pepper

Juice from 1 lemon

2 sprigs thyme, minced

2 sprigs rosemary, minced

INSTRUCTIONS

Preheat oven to 350°F (180°C, or gas mark 4). Rinse chicken and remove giblets. I like to put the giblets in a bag and freeze them until I'm ready to make stock, or you can fry up the livers in a little butter while the chicken is roasting. Place the chicken in a baking dish lined with parchment paper (you can skip the parchment paper but it makes cleanup so much easier). Pat the chicken dry with paper towels and rub with the melted fat then sprinkle with salt, pepper, lemon juice, thyme and rosemary. Place the used lemon inside the chicken cavity along with the herbs. Roast the chicken for approximately 2 hours before checking to see if it's cooked. The best tool for this is a digital instant read thermometer. (Do yourself a favor and get one—resisted forever but it's such a useful tool if you are tired of overcooked and undercooked meats.) The internal temp should be 165°F (74°C) when measured at the thigh. Tip: Don't let the probe touch the bones or it will throw off your reading. The ideal place to insert the thermometer is right at the junction of the leg and the breast, about mid-way up the side of the chicken.

If you don't have a meat thermometer, try these tricks to know when the chicken is cooked enough: Wiggle the leg and see if it could easily be pulled off from the rest of the bird. You can also pierce the thigh meat with a knife and look to see if the juices run clear (as opposed to pinkish which indicates an undercooked bird).

TERRIFIC "TERIYAKI" JERKY

Jerky is excellent for a snack or quick breakfast on the run, but it's very expensive to buy and often has lots of ingredients I don't want to eat. I tried quite a few recipes before I landed on this one that I love. The first time I made jerky, I sliced it way too thin and overdried it, producing crunchy "beef chips." Some of my earlier recipes were too salty; others had too much vinegar or heat in them. This one is just right! If you don't have a dehydrator, check out my friend, Henry Fong's blog: www.fitbomb.com for his creative solution using oven racks and plastic building blocks, like LEGO bricks. To make jerky a full lunch, try serving it with a hard-boiled egg or a handful of nuts and a piece of fruit.

Makes about 2 servings

INGREDIENTS

1 lb (454 g) flank steak

¼ cup (60 ml) coconut aminos

2 tbsp (30 ml) Worcestershire sauce (see Resources)

1 tbsp (15 ml) all natural liquid smoke

1 tbsp (7 g) onion powder

1 tbsp (7 g) garlic powder

¼ tsp cayenne pepper

½ tsp smoked paprika

2 tsp honey

INSTRUCTIONS

Slice the steak against the grain into strips about ⅛ inch (3 mm) thick. Don't worry about slicing them paper thin. (Tip: Slightly frozen meat is a bit easier to slice.) Place the meat in a container or bag with remaining ingredients and marinate overnight. Remove from marinade and place on paper towels to dry. Place either in your dehydrator or on racks in the oven set to the lowest possible setting (*see below*). I like my jerky to be slightly chewy and still a little soft. Check the meat after about 3 hours. Three hours is usually how long it takes for my jerky in a dehydrator set at 155°F (68°C). Remove the jerky and allow to cool to room temperature before storing in refrigerator. If you store it warm, condensation will develop and create moisture on the jerky.

MAKING JERKY IN A CONVENTIONAL OVEN

Preheat your oven to 170°F (75°C). Remember you are not cooking the meat; you are simply dehydrating it. You'll need metal cookie racks or roasting racks rubbed with some coconut oil to prevent sticking. Place a metal baking sheet covered with tinfoil under the racks to catch any drips. Drape the meat over the wire racks and place in the oven. Leave in the oven to dehydrate for about 3 to 4 hours. Check on the jerky regularly to ensure that it doesn't get too dry. You want the jerky to be a deep reddish-brown color and still be flexible.

EASY-PEEL **HARD-BOILED EGGS**

I'm very lucky to have a virtually endless supply of nutrient-dense, fresh, pastured eggs at my disposal from my farm. Fresh eggs don't have a large air sac between the egg white and shell, making them very hard to peel when hard-boiled. Older egg (like the ones you buy at the grocery store) are easier to peel when hard-boiled because as time passes the egg white starts to shrink away from the shell. Even though I love to eat hard-boiled and deviled eggs, I used to spend so long trying to remove the shell that in the end they didn't look appetizing at all. That is, until my friend Liz Wolfe (of Cavegirleats.com) sent me a Twitter message from someone asking how to make them. Someone suggested this simple tip: Add baking soda to the water. I decided to try it for myself and it worked beautifully! My daughter loves hard-boiled eggs, especially when they're sliced with an egg slicer. This magically transforms them into perfectly round coins that she can dip in sea salt. Hard-boiled eggs from pastured hens are a perfect food to take to the office or toss in a lunch box for the kids.

Makes about 3 servings

INGREDIENTS

6 eggs

1 tbsp (18 g) salt

2 tsp baking soda

INSTRUCTIONS

In a medium-sized saucepan, place 6 eggs, salt and baking soda. Bring just to a boil then reduce the heat and allow to lightly simmer for 12 minutes. Place the pot in the sink and drain the water. Shake the pot so the eggshells crack and add cold water. Allow to sit for at least 5 minutes or until the eggs are cool. Peel the eggs. Compost the shells. If you'd like to pack them for later, just skip the shaking part and refrigerate in the unbroken shells. They will peel easily for you when you're ready to eat them.

BAKING YOUR **BACON**

It's amazing to me how many people don't know this simple way to prepare bacon. Once you try it, you'll never go back to pan frying. Preheat your oven to 350°F (180°C, or gas mark 4). Line a baking sheet with parchment paper and lay out the bacon in one single layer, not letting any pieces touch each other. Place in the oven and bake for approximately 20 minutes or until crisp. Remove from the oven and place bacon on a plate lined with paper towels to drain excess bacon fat. Make additional layers of paper towel if necessary. While the pan is still warm and fat is in a liquid state, carefully pour the bacon fat into a glass. Reserve the bacon fat for frying your eggs or vegetables. I like to make a large batch like this and save the bacon in the fridge for meals later in the week. If there happens to be any leftover (unlikely), bacon is excellent cooked with greens like kale, mustard and Swiss chard.

SUNDRIED TOMATO ROSEMARY BISCUITS

All I have to say about these is *wow*. Before I was Paleo and eating a basic gluten-free diet, I was a huge fan of Chebe's Orginal Cheese Bread Mix, a tapioca-based mix that you add tons of cheese to and bake into addictive little starch bombs. You can get these little cheese rolls at Brazilian restaurants too. I tried making a Paleo version with just tapioca and they didn't quite work. Then I tried with other flours mixed in and they were perfect! Have these alongside the Lemon Spinach and Egg Ribbon Soup (page 105) or make a large biscuit with roasted chicken and pesto inside and slice it like a roll.

About 4 servings

INGREDIENTS

½ cup (112 g) ghee, melted

2 eggs

¼ cup (60 ml) water

2 cups (240 g) tapioca starch

⅓ cup (40 g) potato flour

¼ cup (30 g) coconut flour

½ tsp baking soda

½ tsp salt

1 tsp cream of tartar

1 tbsp (1 g) fresh rosemary, minced

4 sundried tomatoes, minced

INSTRUCTIONS

Preheat your oven to 350°F (180°C, or gas mark 4). Combine the ghee, eggs and water in a small bowl. Next, combine the starch, the flours, baking soda, salt and cream of tartar. Mix the dry ingredients well. Combine the wet and dry ingredients and mix in the rosemary and sundried tomatoes. On a baking sheet lined with parchment paper, place golf-ball-sized balls of the dough. Bake for about 18 minutes or until light brown. Don't worry if they are a bit gooey inside from the tapioca starch. Note: Fresh basil and other fresh herbs make great addition to these biscuits, too!

NO-STRESS **HOMEMADE CHICKEN STOCK**

I know making your own stock sounds intimidating, but it's not as hard as you think and it's so much better for you than that canned stuff. I make this magic broth a few times a month. When I'm done feeding my family the meat from a whole chicken, I place the carcass in a freezer bag and save it until I'm ready. I also save the organs and other chicken parts like the feet, which give the broth extra richness and gelatin.

Yields vary but you should get at least 6 to 7 quarts (6 to 7 liters)

INGREDIENTS

4 to 5 quarts (4 to 5 liters) cold filtered water

3 leftover roasted chicken carcasses plus bonus chicken feet and/or organs (optional)

¼ cup (60 ml) cider vinegar

1 large onion

4 carrots, peeled

3 celery stalks

1 tbsp (5 g) peppercorns

3 bay leaves

INSTRUCTIONS

Fill a large stockpot with the cold water and add the chicken and vinegar. Allow to sit for 30 minutes, then bring to a boil and skim any scum that comes to the surface. Add the onion, carrots, celery (no need to chop them), peppercorns and bay leaves then reduce heat to a very low simmer and cover. The longer you cook the stock, the richer it will be. I usually start mine early in the morning and turn off the heat at the end of the day. After you've turned off the heat, allow to cool for about 1 hour on the stovetop. Strain the soup into one large bowl or separate, smaller pots and place in the refrigerator to cool (I usually do this overnight). When the broth is fully cooled, skim off the fat that will have risen to the top and discard it. Ladle stock into freezer-safe containers and store until you're ready to use it.

VARIATIONS:

You can also make stock with a whole raw chicken using this same process. I do this with older laying hens which aren't very tender when roasted and do better going straight into the stockpot.

To make beef/lamb/goat or venison broth, follow the same recipe except use about 6 pounds (2,724 g) of bones. A combination of knucklebones, marrowbones and meaty neck bones or tails will yield a stock rich in flavor and gelatin. Roast the bones in the oven on a baking sheet at 350°F (180°C, or gas mark 4) for about 1 hour, then place the bones and pan drippings into a stockpot with cold water and vinegar. Follow directions above.

SWEET POTATO CREPES
WITH CHIVES

These are way too good to be Paleo! They're like soft little tortillas, which are the perfect vehicle for any number of fillings. I picked up some sweet potato flour one day at a specialty food store and after letting it sit for months in my cabinet was inspired to pull it out and try making some crepes. We like to eat them with day-old pot roast or lamb stew. The crepes make last night's dinner a little more special than "just leftovers." It also makes leftovers extra portable to eat at the office or on the run. They're super simple to make and give you a bread-like accompaniment to any meal.

Makes about 10 crepes

INGREDIENTS

⅓ cup (40 g) sweet potato flour

½ cup (60 g) tapioca starch

½ tsp salt

½ tsp baking soda

1 tsp cream of tartar

3 eggs

1 cup (235 ml) coconut milk

4 tbsp (4 g) minced chives

1 tsp coconut oil for frying

INSTRUCTIONS

Combine all ingredients. If the mixture appears lumpy, just take your immersion blender and blend until smooth. In a skillet over medium-high heat, melt the coconut oil. Working in batches, drop 2 pancake-sized amounts of the batter into the pan. When the top no longer looks raw and the bottom is light brown, flip and continue cooking for another few minutes until brown. Remove from heat.
Tip: Add a teaspoon of curry powder to the batter and wrap these around scrambled eggs for an exciting breakfast wrap!

CHAPTER 7

Snappy Sides

Here are some Paleo side dishes that will round out your meals and satisfy your deepest cravings. Need something to go with that lettuce wrap? No problem! I've got a great "Cheesy" Kale Chip recipe and an incredible technique for the Crunchy Root Chips that will deliver some crunch without the guilt. Miss crackers? I sure did when I first went Paleo. I've not only got a terrific crispy and flavorful cracker recipe, but also two different pâtés you can spread on them.

Looking for something that's a little different than a standard wrap, soup or stew? Try the Thai Curry Crab Cakes to Go or the Salmon and Zucchini Sliders. All you need is a small salad to make these dishes a complete, restaurant-style meal without the common drawback of gluten or unhealthy oils.

SALMON AND ZUCCHINI SLIDERS

These little salmon cakes are full of flavor and easy to make. Serve them with a salad of baby greens dressed with lemon juice and olive oil or drizzle some homemade Lemony Paprika Aioli over the top (page 182). They're portable for an office lunch and also good enough to serve to guests.

Makes 3 servings

INGREDIENTS

2 cups (240 g) shredded zucchini (about 2 medium-sized zucchini)

½ tsp salt

1 lb (454 g) fresh wild salmon

2 tbsp (13 g) chopped fennel

½ lemon, juiced

1 cup (32 g) loosely packed basil leaves, chopped

2 tbsp (2 g) fennel fronds, minced

1 egg

¼ tsp cayenne pepper

2 scallions, minced

1 tsp mustard powder

¼ tsp pepper

1 tbsp (14 g) coconut oil for frying

Another ½ lemon for after they're cooked

INSTRUCTIONS

Grate the zucchini and place in a bowl with the salt. Set aside for ½ hour as the salt removes some of the moisture from the zucchini. In a food processor, add the salmon, fennel, lemon juice and basil. Puree into a paste. Now drain the zucchini by wrapping it in a kitchen towel and squeeze it to remove the water. Pour off the water in the bowl and place the dry zucchini back in. Add to the zucchini the fennel fronds, egg, cayenne, scallions, mustard powder and pepper and mix well. Now incorporate the salmon paste to the zucchini. To cook, warm a skillet over medium heat. Place 1 teaspoon of the coconut oil in the pan and working in batches, place 2-tablespoon clumps of the mixture in the pan. Flip when the bottoms are light brown and continue cooking on the other side until done, about 3 minutes per side. Remove warm cakes to a plate and squeeze a touch of lemon juice over them as they cool.

THAI CURRY CRAB CAKES TO GO

This is one of the best recipes in my book and it's so simple to make, you can't screw it up! I usually keep a can of all-natural crabmeat in my refrigerator just in case I run out of ideas for dinner. In fact, all of the ingredients in this recipe are things I always have on hand. I can whip up these delicious crab cakes at a moment's notice. These little protein-packed nuggets are great to take along to the office or to the gym for a quick post-workout refuel. Crabs are an excellent source of protein, vitamin B12, zinc, copper and selenium.

Makes about 10 crab cakes

INGREDIENTS

FOR THE CRAB CAKES:

2 cups (270 g) all natural white lump crab meat

2 tbsp (30 g) Thai red curry paste

1 tsp sriracha

2 scallions, minced

3 tbsp (3 g) cilantro, minced

1 egg

¼ cup (56 g) Hassle-Free Homemade Mayonnaise (page 180)

½ tsp salt and pepper

½ cup (60 g) potato starch

FOR THE SAUCE:

1 cup (235 ml) coconut milk

Juice from ½ lime

1 tbsp (1 g) cilantro, minced

INSTRUCTIONS

Heat your oven to 350°F (180°C, or gas mark 4). In a large bowl, combine all of the ingredients and mix well. Lay a sheet of parchment paper on a baking sheet and place palm-sized patties on the sheet. I usually get about ten cakes from this recipe. Bake for 25 minutes. While the crab cakes are baking, make your sauce by combining the 3 ingredients in a small bowl. Remove the cooked crab cakes and spoon the sauce over them if you're ready to eat, or simply pack the sauce to dip the crab cakes in later at the office.

Tip: Alternatively, you can lightly oil a pan with 1 tablespoon coconut oil and cook over medium heat for about 5 minutes per side, or until lightly browned.

MOROCCAN MEATBALLS

Good meatballs from my favorite deli are something I initially missed when I first went gluten free. Now I have an even more satisfying replacement! These moist, exotic meatballs have sweet Moroccan flavor from the spices and mint. They can be made for a simple weeknight dinner and the leftovers can be transformed into my Moroccan Meatballs in Sweet Potato Crepes with Chives (page 157) so much healthier and delicious than your local Italian takeout sandwich. You'll never want a classic meatball sub again!

Makes approximately 32 golf-ball-sized meatballs

INGREDIENTS

2 lb (908 g) of ground lamb (substitute dark meat turkey or chicken)

½ onion, minced

4 cloves garlic, minced

2 tsp sundried tomatoes, rehydrated and minced

1 tbsp (7 g) cumin

1 tbsp (7 g) coriander

2 tbsp (4 g) fresh mint

1 tsp ground cloves

½ tsp cayenne pepper

1 egg

salt and pepper

INSTRUCTIONS

Mix all of the meatball ingredients together and form small meatballs, about 2 to 3 tablespoons (28 to 42 g) of meat per meatball. Place them on a baking sheet lined with parchment paper and bake in a 350°F (180°C, or gas mark 4) oven for approximately 15 minutes or until the internal temperature reaches 160°F (71°C). Move the oven rack to the broiler position and place meatballs under the broiler for about 2 minutes or until brown. When done, remove to a plate to cool. You'll need about 9 meatballs per lunch portion. Save the rest of the meatballs for up to a week in the refrigerator.

SUPERHERO **CHICKEN LIVER PÂTÉ**

In order to get my kids to eat something that I really want them to try, I'll sometimes tell them that food will give them superpowers. This pâté won't give you super Jedi life force or extreme night vision, but liver is a Paleo super food. Liver is full of vitamin A (great for eyesight), folate (wonderful for fertility) and selenium (which can help support your thyroid). With the addition of bacon and mushrooms, this pâté is very rich and is perfect served on Sea-Salted Rosemary Chive Crackers (page 175). It also pairs nicely with a soup or light salad.

Makes about 1 ½ quarts (680 g)

INGREDIENTS

1 lb (454 g) naturally raised chicken livers

1 small onion, diced

2 tbsp (28 g) butter plus ½ cup (112 g) butter

1 tbsp (1 g) fresh rosemary

1 tbsp (6 g) dried thyme

8 oz (228 g) crimini mushrooms

½ cup (120 ml) balsamic vinegar

4 cloves garlic

1 tsp Dijon mustard

1 tbsp (15 ml) fresh lemon juice

1 hard-boiled egg

4 strips bacon, broken into bits

3 tbsp (6 g) flat leaf parsley, minced

salt and pepper to taste

INSTRUCTIONS

In a large skillet, sauté the chicken livers and onions in 2 tablespoons (28 g) of butter with the rosemary and thyme until the onions are tender. Add the mushrooms and sauté for about 5 minutes. Next, add the vinegar, garlic and mustard and sauté until the liquid is gone, about 15 minutes. Transfer to a food processor. Add the lemon juice, hard-boiled egg and bacon bits. One tablespoon at a time, add the remaining ½ cup (112 g) butter until smooth. Transfer to a bowl and mix in the parsley, then add salt and pepper to taste. Refrigerate for about 2 hours before serving. Spread on Sea Salted Rosemary Chive Crackers (page 175) or try simply on raw carrots or celery.

Tip: It's worth it to make a special trip to a good butcher or, better yet, a farmer for high-quality chicken livers.

CRUNCHY **ROOT CHIPS**

These chips are a million times more delicious than standard potato chips, and because you're frying them in coconut oil, they're also much healthier! If you're lucky enough to have an ethnic store or section in your local grocery store, see if you can get your hands on yucca, malanga blanca or some batata root. Malanga is also called *yautía* or *Japanese potatoes*—they are very common in Cuban cooking. Yucca root is a little easier to find than the other roots. These will hit the spot when you pair them with one of your favorite wraps for lunch!

Makes 1 to 2 cups (110 to 220 g) of chips (depending on the size of the root you use)

INGREDIENTS

1 Malanga blanca, yucca root or batata root (malanga blanca is my favorite!)

⅓ cup (70 g) coconut oil

salt

INSTRUCTIONS

Peel and slice the root on a mandoline. In a large cast iron skillet with deep sides, heat ½ inch (1.3 cm) of coconut oil over medium high heat. Drop in 10 or so root slices and watch for them to turn light golden brown on the edges and to look cooked in the center. Remove from oil with a slotted spoon and drain on a paper towel. Sprinkle with a pinch of salt while still warm. Be careful not to eat the entire plate while you're waiting for the next batch to cook. Store in a wax paper bag and bring to the office.

ZUCCHINI "PASTA" WITH TOMATO SAUCE

This amazing dish takes only minutes to prepare and is perfect for a night when you want something a little bit special but don't have much time. The addition of sundried tomatoes gives the sauce a deep, rich taste as if it was simmered on the stove for hours. If you're scared of sardines, try this recipe before you decide to write them off forever. They're packed with vitamins A, D and B12 and minerals like calcium, selenium and phosphorus. They're also a great source of omega-3 fatty acids, the fat that helps reduce inflammation. Zucchini pasta makers (also called spiral vegetable slicers) are only about $35 and available online. They produce long, beautiful strips of zucchini and can also be used with lots of other vegetables.

Makes 4 servings

INGREDIENTS

2 medium zucchinis

1 28-oz (784 g) can peeled diced tomatoes (if using fresh, use about 8 plum tomatoes)

¾ cup (24 g) loosely packed fresh basil leaves

¾ cup (82 g) sundried tomatoes packed in oil

1 tsp dried oregano

½ tsp salt

¼ tsp pepper

3 tbsp (45 ml) olive oil

2 (4.3 oz, or 120 g) cans sardines, drained and broken up into small pieces

INSTRUCTIONS

Cut the zucchini on the spiral vegetable slicer. You can also slice it on a mandoline or with a vegetable peeler, making very long, thin strips of the zucchini. Set aside in a bowl. To make the sauce, combine the tomatoes, basil, sundried tomatoes, oregano, salt and pepper and olive oil in a blender and puree until smooth. Remove mixture to a bowl and add the sardines. Toss with the zucchini pasta. If bringing to the office, pack the sauce separately from the zucchini. You can eat the sauce at room temperature or warmed.

Tip: If using fresh tomatoes, here's how to peel them: Cut small Xs in the bottom of the tomatoes. Bring a pot of water to boil on the stove and dunk the tomatoes in the water for about 15 to 30 seconds, then remove to an ice bath. Peel the skins and gently squeeze out any excess moisture. Proceed with the directions above.

BACON AND EGG SALAD
WITH FRESH HERBS

This is absolutely the most amazing egg salad I've ever tasted. I think the key is to use pasture-raised eggs and homemade mayo, and of course not to overcook the eggs. The fresh herbs and lemon juice brighten it up and the bacon makes it extra dreamy. I love to serve this for farm guests inside a large, stripped German tomato or other heirloom tomato when fresh herbs are in abundance. Kids love it served in hollowed-out cucumbers (make little "cups" in the cucumber with a melon baller). This is not your grandma's egg salad! I guarantee you'll be impressed, so give it a try.

Makes about 4 servings

INGREDIENTS

8 pasture-raised eggs

1 tsp baking soda

1 tsp salt

2 tbsp (4 g) minced fresh parsley

2 tbsp (4 g) minced fresh basil

1 tbsp (1 g) minced fresh chives

2 tbsp (20 g) minced red onion

⅓ cup (75 g) Hassle-Free Homemade Mayonnaise (page 180)

1 tbsp (11 g) plus 1 tsp Dijon mustard

1 tsp fresh lemon juice

2 strips of bacon, crumbled

salt and pepper to taste

INSTRUCTIONS

To hard-boil the eggs, fill a medium-sized pot with water and bring to a boil. Reduce to a simmer and add 1 teaspoon baking soda and 1 teaspoon salt. Gently add the eggs with a slotted spoon and simmer lightly for 14 minutes. When done, drain the pot and crack the eggs against the side of the pot by shaking it. Add cold water and allow to sit while you chop the herbs and onion. Peel the eggs and place in a bowl. Using a pastry cutter or your hands, break up the eggs into small chunks. Add the herbs, mayo, mustard, lemon juice, onion and bacon. Season with salt and pepper to taste.

Tip: Serve on Sea-Salted Rosemary Chive Crackers (page 175), in lettuce leaves, or for a stunning presentation, a hollowed-out heirloom tomato.

"CHEESY" KALE CHIPS

No need for chips in seed oils—these kale chips do the trick for adults and kids! Impress your vegan friends at the next potluck with these crunchy and addictive treats. Vegans love nutritional yeast because it has a cheesy flavor and it's high in B vitamins, especially B12 which is typically lacking in a vegan diet (without supplementation). Be sure you don't mistake nutritional yeast for brewer's yeast: They look similar, but most brewer's yeast is grown on beer and is not considered gluten free. Nutritional yeast tastes pretty good, so give it a chance: It has a cheesy flavor that is really appealing, especially if you are dairy free. Pack these nutrient-dense chips with your lunch for that salty crunch that we Paleo folks often miss. For variations, try adding a small amount of cayenne pepper to the yeast, or sprinkle with cider vinegar and extra salt for salt and vinegar chips.

Makes about 2 servings

INGREDIENTS

1 bunch of kale (I like the curly variety for this recipe but any type will do)

1 tbsp (15 ml) melted coconut oil

¼ cup (30 g) nutritional yeast

salt and pepper to taste

INSTRUCTIONS

Preheat the oven to 350°F (180°C, or gas mark 4). Line 2 baking trays with parchment paper. Set aside. Tear the kale into small, bite-sized pieces, discarding the middle stalk. Wash and dry it well. In a large bowl, mix the kale with the coconut oil, massaging it well to coat each piece. Put the nutritional yeast on a small plate. Dip each kale piece in the nutritional yeast then place the kale on the baking sheet. Sprinkle with a touch salt and pepper, if desired. Bake for approximately 5 to 7 minutes. Watch these carefully in the oven because they can burn really easily. You want to see them dry but not brown. Remove from oven and allow to cool. Once cooled, you can store them in wax paper snack bags.

INDIAN-SPICED ROASTED
WINTER SQUASH

In the fall and winter, this is my go-to side dish for breakfast, lunch and dinner.
I much prefer the taste of winter squash to sweet potatoes. The texture is a bit lighter
and I think the flavor is more interesting. I've been making this dish for about ten years
and always impress myself! If you don't have delicata, substitute another winter squash.
Take this hash and puree it with coconut milk to make a great lunchtime soup,
or add it to some stock, tomatoes and meat for a rich stew.

Makes 3 to 4 servings

INGREDIENTS

**2 delicata squash, peeled and
seeded (substitute 1 medium
butternut or other similar-sized
squash)**

4 cloves garlic, minced

½ tsp salt

¼ tsp pepper

1 tsp cumin

1 tsp coriander

¼ tsp cinnamon

**2 tbsp (30 ml) melted ghee or
coconut oil**

INSTRUCTIONS

Preheat oven to 350°F (180°C, or gas mark 4). Line a baking sheet
with parchment paper. Dice the squash into 2-inch (5 cm) cubes.
Combine all ingredients in a bowl then lay out on the baking sheet.
Roast for approximately 30 minutes or until you can easily pierce
the squash with a fork.

PORTABLE PRIMAL
SMOKED TROUT PÂTÉ

Here's another pâté but instead of liver, this one uses smoked trout. It's a lovely (and quick) lunch option with the addition of a soup or garden salad. I've even served this as an appetizer to guests and they absolutely raved about it. This briny and fresh-tasting pâté has a refreshing lemony taste and goes really well on the Sea-Salted Rosemary Chive Crackers. No special kitchen appliances are needed to make this: just a mixing bowl and a fork.

Makes about 2 cups (450 g)

INGREDIENTS

1 8-oz (228 g) package smoked trout (I like Ducktrap brand)

1 8-oz (228 g) package of crème fraîche

½ cup (8 g) fresh dill, minced

3 tbsp (24 g) capers, rinsed

¼ red onion, minced

1 tsp pepper

½ lemon, juiced

INSTRUCTIONS

Combine all ingredients in a bowl. Serve with Sea-Salted Rosemary Chive Crackers (page 175). See Smoked Trout Pâté at bottom center. To make Superhero Chicken Liver Pâté (top left), see page 163.

SEA-SALTED ROSEMARY CHIVE CRACKERS

These crackers are to die for! They're crunchy, salty and extremely flavorful. I had never thought of making my own crackers until I saw a recipe in *Paleo Indulgences* by Tammy Credicott. Her recipe calls for almond flour, which I swapped out for tapioca starch. I also added some more seasonings. The trick to making these delicious treats is to roll them very thin. I served these with chicken liver pâté to Diane Sanfilippo and Liz Wolfe when they were in town for a Balanced Bites workshop—so you know I have a lot of confidence in them. Feel free to play around with the herbs to come up with your own creation. Fresh basil, mint, tarragon or thyme would also work well here. They're sure to be a hit.

Makes about 2 servings

INGREDIENTS

1 cup (120 g) tapioca starch

½ cup (60 g) coconut flour

½ tsp sea salt

½ tsp pepper

1 tbsp (1 g) fresh rosemary

1 tbsp (1 g) fresh chives

½ tsp onion powder

½ tsp garlic powder

2 eggs

2 tbsp (30 ml) melted ghee

2 Tbsp (30 ml) water

A little extra sea salt to sprinkle on top

INSTRUCTIONS

Preheat the oven to 350°F (180°C, or gas mark 4). In a medium-sized bowl, combine the tapioca starch, coconut flour, salt, pepper, herbs, onion powder and garlic powder well. Add the eggs, ghee and water and mix with your hands to form a dough ball. Line a baking sheet with parchment paper and place the dough ball on the baking sheet. Flatten the ball with your hands. Cover with waxed paper and with a rolling pin; roll until the ball is very thin, about ¼-inch (6 mm) thick. Sprinkle with a small amount of salt, if desired. With a sharp knife, score the dough into 2 x 2-inch (5 x 5 cm) squares and place on a baking sheet lined with parchment paper. Bake for approximate 15 minutes or until the crackers are lightly browned. You may have to remove some of the thinner, outer crackers early to prevent burning. Store in an airtight container.

ROASTED **DELICATA SQUASH**

This is a great side dish for any meal but also a terrific stuffing for a grab-and-go style lettuce wrap. Just add protein and a little fat, like in the Roasted Chicken, Delicata Squash and Bacon Wrap (page 60). Delicata squash tastes similar to a sweet potato but has about half of the calories. It's also a very good source of vitamins A and C as well as potassium and manganese.

Makes about 4 servings

INGREDIENTS

2 delicata squash

1 tbsp (14 g) coconut oil

1 tbsp (7 g) ground sage

1 tsp pepper

½ tsp salt

½ tsp red pepper flakes

INSTRUCTIONS

Preheat oven to 350°F (180°C, or gas mark 4). Slice the squash and remove the seeds. Remove the outer skin then slice into ½-inch (1.3 cm) pieces. Place the squash in a bowl and add the coconut oil, sage, pepper, salt and red pepper flakes. Combine well and spread the mixture onto a baking sheet lined with parchment paper. Roast for 45 minutes or until lightly browned and tender.

CHAPTER 8

Day-to-Day Dressings

Store-bought salad dressings can be full of rancid industrial oils and all kinds of chemicals. The recipes here will take your meals to a whole new level using much healthier ingredients. My Hassle-Free Homemade Mayonnaise is so much more delicious than what you can buy in a jar. Add it to your favorite weekday wrap and savor the difference it makes. Pour my simple but incredibly delicious Happy Valley Ranch Salad Dressing or my Dreamy Creamy Herb Dressing over your favorite Paleo salad and enjoy!

CREAMY CASHEW
GADO GADO SAUCE

When I first met my husband Andrew, he was nineteen and had just returned from a semester camping in the Rocky Mountains—in the winter with no tents!—through NOLS (National Outdoor Leadership School). He told me that in order to take in enough calories, he and his fellow campers would make bacon and pour the fat on the snow, then eat it as bacon-fat popsicles. Another dish they ate often was pasta with gado gado sauce—a peanut sauce. I've altered the recipe over the years but this is still one of our go-to sauces for meat, salads or zucchini pasta. It's got just a little heat, so if you prefer it spicy you should double the amount of red pepper flakes. I use an immersion blender to make this but a real blender or food processor works just as well.

About 2 cups (470 ml)

INGREDIENTS

1 cup (235 ml) full-fat coconut milk

⅔ cup (170 g) cashew butter

1 clove garlic

¼ tsp red pepper flakes

1 lime, juiced

2 tbsp (30 ml) plus 1 tsp (5 ml) coconut aminos

1 scallion, sliced

2 tbsp (2 g) cilantro, chopped

1 heaping tsp fresh ginger, chopped

INSTRUCTIONS

Combine all ingredients in a blender or a quart (liter) container with an immersion blender. Store the sauce in the refrigerator for up to 1 week. Allow to come to room temperature or heat slightly before using as mixture will solidify in the fridge.

HASSLE-FREE
HOMEMADE MAYONNAISE

It may seem like an inconvenience to make it yourself, but once you have tried homemade mayonnaise, you'll never eat the jarred stuff again. The mayo you find at the grocery store is usually made with "healthy" canola oil, which is not a good fat source because it becomes rancid from the high heat used during the processing of it. This homemade mayonnaise is creamy and rich and only takes about five minutes. One batch can keep in the fridge for a week, so you can have it on hand to embellish your weekday wraps. It can be made even more flavorful by adding fresh herbs, extra lemon juice, extra mustard or some chipotle peppers. I like to make this in a plastic quart (liter) container with a handheld immersion blender but you can also use a food processor or hand whisk instead.

Makes about 2 cups (470 ml)

INGREDIENTS

2 egg yolks

1 tsp Dijon mustard

½ a lemon, juiced

1 cup (235 ml) olive oil

salt and pepper to taste

INSTRUCTIONS

Place the egg yolks, mustard and lemon juice in a plastic quart (liter) container. With the immersion blender, blend the egg and mustard together then *slowly* add the olive oil in a drizzle stream as you blend. The mixture will become thick. Resist the urge to dump the entire amount of olive oil in too quickly, as the mayo will separate. The whole process may take about 5 minutes. When all of the olive oil has been added, add some salt and pepper.

HAPPY VALLEY
RANCH SALAD DRESSING

This tastes exactly like you remember, really! It's named after one of my favorite places in the world, the Amherst/Northampton area of Western Massachusetts where I went to college. Those who live there affectionately call it the Happy Valley. Because the ingredients are healthier than most store-bought dressings, eating this should make you very happy. The idea for the dressing came from my eight-year-old who told me that if I gave him some ranch salad dressing, he would happily eat salad for school lunch. I shivered at the thought of commercial ranch dressing with all of the bad oils and added chemicals. The very next morning I came up with this recipe. It's fast and easy to make, so you can fit it into your busy lifestyle. Use it as a salad dressing, a dip for raw carrots and chicken wings or in a wrap sandwich. Add a bit of cayenne to heat it up if you wish.

Makes about ⅔ cups (150 ml)

INGREDIENTS

2 tbsp (2 g) chives
1 tbsp (1 g) dill
1 large clove garlic
1 tbsp (10 g) diced onion
2 tbsp (4 g) parsley
¼ tsp paprika (use smoked paprika for a smoky ranch dressing)
¼ cup (56 g) Hassle-Free Homemade Mayonnaise (page 180)
¼ cup (60 ml) coconut milk
1 tbsp (15 ml) fresh lemon juice
1 tsp Worcestershire sauce (see Resources)
salt and pepper to taste

INSTRUCTIONS

In a blender or container that you can use an immersion blender in, add all ingredients. Blend until smooth. Store for one week in the refrigerator.

Tip: When packing this dressing for work, allow it to sit at room temperature for about 1 hour prior to pouring the dressing. Otherwise, it will be pretty solid in the refrigerator from the fat in the coconut milk.

MACADAMIA LEMON PESTO

This lemony pesto sauce is perfect for my Portable Tuscan Wrap (page 31), or tossed with zucchini "pasta" noodles cut on a spiral vegetable slicer. I also adore pesto on grilled vegetables and over sliced heirloom tomatoes.

Makes about 1 ½ cups (390 g) of pesto

INGREDIENTS

2 cups (64 g) packed basil leaves

1 cup (145 g) unsalted macadamia nuts

½ tsp finely ground salt

⅛ tsp pepper

Juice of ½ lemon

1 clove garlic

1 cup (235 ml) olive oil

INSTRUCTIONS

Place all ingredients except the olive oil in a food processor and pulse until chopped well. Add the olive oil and process until smooth. Taste for salt and add more to your taste, if needed.

LEMONY PAPRIKA AIOLI

This sauce goes great paired with vegetables or fish. Try it with the Salmon and Zucchinni Sliders (page 159).

Makes about 1 cup (240 ml)

INGREDIENTS

1 egg yolk

1 tsp Dijon mustard

¾ cup (180 ml) olive oil

1 ½ tsp minced garlic

1 ½ tsp ground sweet paprika

½ tsp salt

2 tbsp (30 ml) lemon juice

INSTRUCTIONS

In a medium bowl, whisk together the egg yolk and mustard. Continue whisking while slowly adding the olive oil in a very light stream until the mixture emulsifies. When you've used up all of the olive oil, stir in the garlic, paprika, salt and lemon juice. Serve in a small bowl or drizzle over the Salmon and Zucchini Sliders.

SAUERKRAUT MADE SIMPLE

I always have some sauerkraut in the fridge or some fermenting on my counter. Making it used to seem intimidating but now I do it all the time. As long as you have the ingredients you need and a quart (liter)-sized mason jar, it's a fairly simple process. Numerous ancient cultures have used lacto-fermentation to preserve and actually improve the digestibility and nutrient density of their foods. From ancient China and Japan to Rome and the Middle East, cultures have long been lacto-fermenting their foods and beverages. Even Captain Cook loaded barrels of sauerkraut onto his ship to help prevent scurvy during the voyage. Lactic acid, produced by beneficial bacterial like lactobacillus casei, inhibits the other bacteria that cause putrefaction. Used as a condiment with your favorite Paleo meal, a few tablespoons of uncooked sauerkraut are a great supplement of good bacteria plus an extra boost of vitamins and minerals.

About 1 quart (568 g)

INGREDIENTS

You'll need a quart (liter)-sized mason jar with a lid

1 medium cabbage, outer leaves removed, cored and shredded

2 tbsp (36 g) salt

1 carrot, peeled and grated

2 cloves garlic, minced

½ onion, thinly sliced

½ cup (22 g) arame seaweed, broken into small pieces

INSTRUCTIONS

In a large bowl, mix cabbage with salt. Massage with your hands firmly for about 10 minutes, or until you see water coming from the mixture. Incorporate the other ingredients and mix well. Place in a quart (liter)-sized mason jar and press down firmly until the juices are covering the cabbage. The top of the mixture should be at least 1 inch (2.5 cm) below the jar. Seal the jar and keep at room temperature for at least 3 days and up to 2 weeks before transferring to the refrigerator. Sauerkraut improves with age.

DREAMY **CREAMY HERB DRESSING**

This dressing is perfect with grilled zucchini and fennel or in a turkey wrap. It's creamy but fresh tasting with a little salt from the anchovy paste. Don't be intimidated by the list of ingredients. It only takes a few minutes to make and I guarantee it's worth trying!

Makes about 1 ½ cups (370 ml)

INGREDIENTS

¾ cup (24 g) chopped parsley

2 tbsp (4 g) fresh-chopped basil

1 clove garlic, chopped

3 green onions, chopped

1 tbsp (15 ml) red wine vinegar

1 tbsp (15 ml) fresh lemon juice

½ cup (120 ml) full-fat coconut milk

⅓ cup (75 g) Hassle-Free Homemade Mayonnaise (page 180)

INSTRUCTIONS

Place all ingredients in a blender and blend until smooth. Store in the refrigerator for up to 1 week.

Tip: When packing this dressing for work, allow to sit at room temperature for about 1 hour prior to pouring the dressing. Otherwise, it will be pretty solid in the refrigerator from the fat in the coconut milk.

Resources

CONDIMENTS YOU CAN PURCHASE

I haven't yet tasted good store-bought Paleo mayonnaises or salad dressings available for purchase. Because of this, I feel pretty strongly about making your own. You can get away with swapping out some other condiments as long as the rest of your diet is clean and you're not going to drink it by the gallon. One teaspoon of gluten-free Worcestershire sauce with a little sugar in it, for example, is not the end of the world. If you want to stay purely Paleo but you don't have the time to make all your condiments at home, here are some recommended products for purchase:

BBQ SAUCE

Most BBQ sauce is loaded with high-fructose corn syrup. Luckily there's a great one on the market and it's a 100% Paleo-compliant version. **PaleoChef Peach BBQ by Steve's PaleoGoods** is available online and the ingredients are clean. Looking to make your own? The Food Lovers Kitchen has a delicious tangy barbeque sauce recipe on their website that I recommend you try if you're going to smother some ribs.

SARDINES

Look for sardines labeled "Pacific" (not Atlantic, which are actually often caught in the Mediterranean, and have been overfished). I like **Wild Planet brand sardines** packed in olive oil, and they use BPA-Free cans. There are other canned fish products like salmon, tuna and crab meat that are also great.

SAUERKRAUT

Wildbrine and **Real Pickles** are two of my favorite brands of naturally fermented sauerkraut. If you're not going to make your own, then these products are a nice alternative.

SRIRACHA

Look for **Lee Kum Kee brand Sriracha Chili Sauce.** It does contain sugar, but it doesn't have a lot of the terrible chemical preservatives that most traditional sriracha products have. I found it at my local Whole Foods. You can also find **Jalapeño Pepper Hot Sauce at Trader Joe's** that only has red jalapenos, vinegar and salt. It doesn't have the same sweetness as sriracha, but it doesn't have the sugar. If you'd like to make it yourself, check out nomnompaleo.com for Michelle Tam's homemade sriracha sauce. It's amazing.

WORCESTERSHIRE SAUCE

Lea & Perrins brand (yes the traditional kind that you grew up eating) is gluten free but has some sugar in it. I also like the taste of it. If you'd like to make your own, check out fastpaleo.com for a great recipe called "Easy Homemade Worcestershire Sauce."

FISH SAUCE

Red Boat brand is an excellent choice if you are looking for Paleo-friendly fish sauce.

NUTRITION/LIFESTYLE BOOKS

The Paleo Solution by Robb Wolf

The Primal Blueprint by Mark Sisson

Practical Paleo by Diane Sanfilippo

It Starts with Food by Dallas and Melissa Hartwig

Modern Cave Girl: Paleo Living in The Concrete Jungle by Liz Wolfe

Naked Calories: How Micronutrients Can Maximize Weight Loss, Prevent Disease and Enhance Your Life by Mira Calton and Jayson Calton

Perfect Health Diet: Regain Health and Lose Weight by Eating the Way You Were Meant to Eat by Paul Jaminet and Shou-Ching Jaminet

The Vegetarian Myth: Food, Justice and Sustainability by Lierre Keith

Lights Out: Sleep, Sugar, and Survival by T. S. Wiley with Bent Formby

PALEO COOKBOOKS

I love collecting traditional cookbooks and adapting recipes to my dietary restrictions. Books like *The Joy of Cooking* and other classics are very valuable. I also love reading vegetarian cookbooks for more interesting ways to prepare greens and other vegetables. Here are some recommended cookbooks for Paleo eaters:

Make it Paleo by Bill Staley and Hayley Mason

Gather by Hayley Mason and Bill Staley

Well Fed: Paleo Recipes for People Who Love to Eat by Melissa Joulwan

Paleo Comfort Foods by Julie and Charles Mayfield

The Primal Blueprint Cookbook by Mark Sisson

Eat Well, Feel Good: Practical Paleo Living by Diane Frampton

Everyday Paleo by Sarah Fragoso

Paleo Indulgences by Tammy Credicott

BLOGS AND OTHER WEBSITES

My personal business website, www.radiancenutrition.com and my blog, www. sustainabledish.com are places I suggest you visit if you like this book and are looking for more info on food, nutrition and my experiences as a mom, student and living on a farm. If you'd like to learn more about my farm, visit www.clarkfarmcarlisle.com.

Robb Wolf (robbwolf.com)

After talking with Robb Wolf about my interest in getting the word out about sustainability issues to the public, he encouraged me to start my blog, Sustainable Dish. Robb is also the one who suggested I return to school to become a registered dietitian. His book, *The Paleo Solution*, is really what turned my life around and fixed my metabolic derangement. He has a terrific blog and extremely entertaining podcast that I never miss.

Chris Kresser (chriskresser.com)

Chris Kresser is an acupuncturist in the San Francisco area who also sees people long distance via phone and Skype. I turn to his podcasts to get in-depth information about alternative medicine issues. He really knows his stuff and is always up on the latest research.

Mark's Daily Apple (www.marksdailyapple.com)

This is a fantastic resource for all things "primal." Get recipes, exercise and lifestyle tips from Mark Sisson.

Nom Nom Paleo (nomnomPaleo.com)

This is the best recipe blog out there. A fellow mom looking to feed her family the most nutrient-dense foods she can get her hands on, Michelle Tam blogs each day and has won Saveur's Best Special Diets Blog award. Her posts are informative and funny, and the photographs are amazing. She recently launched an iPad application with step-by-step instructions on how to recreate her recipes.

Fitbomb (www.fitbomb.com)

"Fitbomb," as Henry Fong calls himself, is the other half of the Nom Nom Paleo team. He has a great blog about fitness, health and other interesting posts in parenting and just life. Check it out.

Evolutionary Psychiatry (evolutionarypsychiatry. blogspot.com)

Emily Deans, a fellow Boston-ite and mother, is a psychiatrist and runs a blog connecting food and mental health. I'm extremely interested and passionate about this topic as I feel that more than half of my job as a nutritionist is actually trying to figure out how to motivate people to change.

Balanced Bites (balancedbites.com)

Diane Sanfilippo of Balanced Bites was the first practitioner I called when I started my own nutrition practice. She gave me some terrific advice and continues to inspire me. I've had the honor of being her guest on her fabulous podcast. I also very much appreciate all of the client referrals Diane has passed my way, as she has become busy with her books, podcast and other projects.

Cave Girl Eats (cavegirleats.com)

Liz Wolfe, co hosts the Balanced Bites Podcast with Diane Sanfilippo. She graduated from the same nutrition program that I attended, Nutritional Therapy Association, and runs the popular blog, Cave Girl Eats, and just wrote *Modern Cave Girl*. Liz is smart, funny and has been a great colleague for me to bounce ideas off.

The Food Lovers Kitchen (www.primal-palate.com)

Bill and Hayley are the couple behind The Food Lovers Kitchen. I met them at the PaleoFX conference when we all shared a house with a handful of other bloggers. They have three beautiful cookbooks, *Make it Paleo, Gather,* and *The 30 Day Guide to Paleo Cooking*; an e-book, *The 30 Day Intro to Paleo*; plus a website full of delicious and nutrient dense foods. Bill is also a talented photographer and shot the cover photo for my blog.

Paleo Parents (paleoparents.com)

Stacy Toth and Matt McCarry together have lost over 200 pounds on the Paleo Diet. They've got two books out: *Eat Like a Dinosaur* and *Beyond Bacon*. Their blog is full of great gluten-free recipes that kids will love.

Ancestralize Me! (www.ancestralizeme.com)

Laura is a graduate student at the University of North Carolina at Chapel Hill, pursuing a Masters in Public Health Nutrition (MPH-RD) and runs the blog, Ancestralize Me! Her insightful posts always impress me.

Civilized Caveman Cooking Creations (civilizedcavemancooking.com)

This is a site run by George Bryant. His recipes are unique, intriguing and beautifully shot (he's also a photographer). It's amazing to me that he can fit in so much cooking while on active duty in the United States Marine Corps. He also has an e-book: *Caveman Feast* available on his site.

Chowstalker (chowstalker.com)

This is your link to the amazingly wide world of Paleo bloggers. These are real folks out there making nutrient-dense food on a daily basis and submitting their meals to this website. I love browsing this site when I am fresh out of ideas for what to cook.

The Foodee Project (www.thefoodee.com)

I've got a "meal of the day" widget link to this site from my nutrition site and I love seeing the new photos every day. It features nicely organized Paleo recipes that you can save and organize, and even create a shopping list.

Acknowledgements

There are some folks in the Paleo community who have really reached out to me and have helped me immensely. Robb Wolf, whose book has changed my health forever, has been so supportive and encouraging. Diane Sanfilippo has been extremely helpful and inclusive, introducing me to others in the community and encouraging me to seek out a mentor. This brings me to Mat Lalonde, who is the ace up my sleeve. He's been incredibly patient with all of my academic questions and has guided me with my nutrition practice and education. Another key person in my education has been Amy Kubal, who has been so upbeat and helpful to me from the minute I met her. I'd also like to offer huge thanks to Bill Staley and Hayley Mason for taking photos for my Sustainable Dish blog and producing beautiful videos of my farm during the Sustainable Feast Dinner and the weekend after. Even though Michelle Tam and Henry Fong almost burnt down my house, they are terrific and have been incredibly inspiring friends. And to Chris Kresser, Liz Wolfe, Stacy Toth, Laura Schoenfeld, and all of the others I've met in the Paleo world who have been so warm and welcoming to me.

Thanks to Will and the team at Page Street Publishing, who made this process smooth and easy. I appreciate all of the positive feedback and gentle nudges to make sure I was producing my very best work. I'm so thrilled with the finished product and this wouldn't have happened without you.

Sincere thanks to Justin Keane at CrossFit Woodshed for brainstorming recipes with me and helping me to make friends with back squats.

To Marjie Findlay, Geoff Freeman, Frank Proctor and everyone else involved with Clark Farm. I absolutely love the energy around this magical farm and it comes from the people involved here. I wake up every morning and look out over the most beautiful place on earth. I'm so incredibly grateful for the honor of taking care of this piece of history, and giving back to the community a relationship to nourishing food.

Thank you to the Rodgers Family for taking me in as another child and showing your love and support through my adult life.

To my dad, who was always cooking something really big in my house growing up, you have been such a light in my life. You gave me a great sense of adventure with food. I'll always remember going clamming as a kid on the beaches of Shinnecock Bay and cooking the clams right there in a fire on the sand. You've always been so incredibly supportive of everything I do. I love you very much. Mom, thanks for taking me to museums, art classes and instilling in me a love for the natural sciences from a very young age.

The biggest hero in my life is my amazing husband Andrew who decided in his mid-twenties to do something completely different with his life, honoring his environmental ideals. We've never looked back. His becoming a sustainable farmer was the hardest and absolute best choice he could have ever made. I couldn't imagine raising our two beautiful children in any other way. Thanks for testing every dish in this book, and for your encouragement and support. Your integrity and endless love for me keeps me strong. Thank you, my love.

About the Author

Diana Rodgers is the founder of Radiance Nutritional Therapy, where she works with people across the country to restore their health with ancestral foods and lifestyle changes. She runs cooking classes, conducts workshops and is the nutrition consultant to several CrossFit gyms. She also runs the blog Sustainable Dish exploring the optimal foods for nutrition, ethical, political and environmental implications. Diana resides on an organic farm with her husband and two children in Carlisle, Massachusetts.

Index

A

apples
Coconut Crepes with Warm Spiced Apples, 18, 75, 76, 137
Sweet Apple Spice Breakfast Sausages, 18, 132
Sweet Potato Apple-Cinnamon Pancakes, 18, 127
Turkey Apple Bacon Wrap with Lemon Herb Sauce, 44
apricots
Smoked Duck Wrap with Cherries and Hazelnuts, 40
Turkey Apricot Dijon Wrap, 34
Asian Chicken "Noodle" Bowl, 92
avocados
Avocado, Orange and Herb Chicken Wrap, 39
Chicken Avocado Bacon Salad, 99
Chicken, Vegetable and Avocado Soup, 18, 109
Crisp Veggie and Turkey Rollup, 18, 38
Hearts of Palm, Shrimp and Avocado Salad, 91
Pulled Pork Wrap with Sauerkraut and Avocado, 26, 75
Spicy Crab, Avocado and Grapefruit Nori Rolls, 43
Spicy Shrimp Salad Wrap, 63
Turkey Avocado and Spicy Pepper Wrap, 58

B

bacon
Bacon and Egg Salad with Fresh Herbs, 18, 167
Bacon and Egg Wrap with Sundried Tomato, 35
Bacon, Lemon and Greens Egg Muffins, 18, 26, 138
Baking Your Bacon, 153
Bubble and Squeak Fried Potato Cakes, 142
Chicken and Peach Firecracker Wrap, 28
Chicken Avocado Bacon Salad, 99
Lamb Tzatziki Gyros in Coconut Crepes, 80
Pineapple Bacon and Chicken Wrap, 52
Roasted Chicken, Delicata Squash and Bacon Wrap, 60
Superhero Chicken Liver Pâté, 163
Turkey Apple Bacon Wrap with Lemon Herb Sauce, 44
Turkey Apricot Dijon Wrap, 34
beef
Cinnamon Beef in a Sweet Potato Pocket, 64
Creamy Indian Goat Curry, 112
Fiery Sweet Dumpling Chili, 106
Lamb "Dosa" Purses with Coconut Crème, 70–72
Pastrami and Pickles in Radicchio Wrap, 55
Roast Beef and Celeriac Slaw Wrap, 49
Roast Beef and Tomato Wrap with Ginger Sauce, 53
Steak Salad with Curry Pickled Vegetables, 100
Tangy Roast Beef and Beets Wrap, 37
Terrific "Teriyaki" Jerky, 18, 151
Two-Minute Steak, Egg and Endive Salad, 82
beets
Lemon, Chive, Beet and Boiled Egg Wrap, 45
Tangy Roast Beef and Beets Wrap, 37

Winter Beet Salad with Orange and Fennel, 26, 96
Blueberry Cinnamon Coconut Smoothie, 18, 26, 146
Brazilian Fish Stew (Moqueca de Peixe), 26, 115
breakfasts
Bacon, Lemon and Greens Egg Muffins, 18, 26, 138
Bubble and Squeak Fried Potato Cakes, 142
Cherry Tarragon Breakfast Sausages, 121
Coconut Crepes with Warm Spiced Apples, 18, 75, 76, 137
Crabby Morning Egg Muffins, 125
Curried Green Eggs and Ham, 26, 122
Ginger and Spice Breakfast Sausages, 119
Ginger Scallion Sweet Potato Cakes, 133
Herbed Omelet with Truffle Butter, 128
Homemade Mexican Chorizo Sausage, 76, 124
Lamb Sausage with Peppers and Herbs, 131
Pear, Sage and Fennel Morning Sausages, 132
Poached Egg with Tuscan Breakfast Hash, 141
Sweet Apple Spice Breakfast Sausages, 18, 132
Sweet Potato Apple-Cinnamon Pancakes, 18, 127
Tortilla Española with Chorizo, 134
Bubble and Squeak Fried Potato Cakes, 142
Butternut Parsnip Soup with Leeks, 116

C

Cajun Fish Po' Boy Wrap, 66
carrots
Asian Chicken "Noodle" Bowl, 92
Chicken, Vegetable and Avocado Soup, 18, 109
Chinese Ginger Pork Wrap, 77
Creamy Indian Goat Curry, 112
Crisp Veggie and Turkey Rollup, 18, 38
No-Stress Homemade Chicken Stock, 103, 156
Orange Fennel Carrot Soup, 103
Sauerkraut Made Simple, 75, 79, 183
Steak Salad with Curry Pickled Vegetables, 100
Vietnamese "Bun" with Pork Teriyaki, 18, 85
"Cheesy" Kale Chips, 18, 168
cherries
Cherry Tarragon Breakfast Sausages, 26, 121
Smoked Duck Wrap with Cherries and Hazelnuts, 40
chicken
Asian Chicken "Noodle" Bowl, 92
Avocado, Orange and Herb Chicken Wrap, 39
Chicken and Peach Firecracker Wrap, 28
Chicken Avocado Bacon Salad, 99
Chicken, Celeriac and Mustard Salad Wrap, 32
Chicken Cranberry Salad and Fennel Wrap, 46
Chicken, Vegetable and Avocado Soup, 18, 109
Lemon Chicken and Veggie Wrap, 50
Lemon Pepper Roasted Chicken, 149
Lemon Spinach & Egg Ribbon Soup, 105
Moroccan Meatballs, 162
No-Stress Homemade Chicken Stock, 103, 156
Pineapple Bacon and Chicken Wrap, 52
Roasted Chicken, Delicata Squash and Bacon Wrap, 60

Superhero Chicken Liver Pâté, 163
Chinese Ginger Pork Wrap, 77
Cinnamon Beef in a Sweet Potato Pocket, 64
Clark Farm, 21, 22–23
Coconut Crepes with Warm Spiced Apples, 18, 75, 76, 137
Cosmopolitan Turkey Salad and Pear Wrap, 57
Crabby Morning Egg Muffins, 125
Creamy Cashew Gado Gado Sauce, 18, 92, 100, 178
Creamy Indian Goat Curry, 112
Crisp Veggie and Turkey Rollup, 18, 38
Crunchy Root Chips, 164
cucumbers
Asian Chicken "Noodle" Bowl, 92
Chicken Avocado Bacon Salad, 99
Crisp Veggie and Turkey Rollup, 18, 38
Lemon Chicken and Veggie Wrap, 50
Peppery Smooth Gazpacho, 113
Spicy Salmon and Cucumber "Noodle" Salad, 87
Vietnamese "Bun" with Pork Teriyaki, 18, 85
Curried Green Eggs and Ham, 26, 122

D

Dreamy Creamy Herb Dressing, 38, 184
dressings
Creamy Cashew Gado Gado Sauce, 18, 92, 100, 178
Dreamy Creamy Herb Dressing, 38, 184
Happy Valley Ranch Salad Dressing, 18, 99, 181
Hassle-Free Homemade Mayonnaise, 180
Lemony Paprika Aioli, 182
Macadamia Lemon Pesto, 182
Sauerkraut Made Simple, 75, 79, 183
duck. See Smoked Duck Wrap with Cherries and Hazelnuts.

E

Easy-Peel Hard-Boiled Eggs, 152
Effortless Egg Rolls with Pickled Vegetables, 79
eggplant. See Grilled Eggplant RollUps.
eggs
Bacon and Egg Salad with Fresh Herbs, 18, 167
Bacon and Egg Wrap with Sundried Tomato, 35
Bacon, Lemon and Greens Egg Muffins, 18, 26, 138
Crabby Morning Egg Muffins, 125
Easy-Peel Hard-Boiled Eggs, 152
Effortless Egg Rolls with Pickled Vegetables, 79
Herbed Omelet with Truffle Butter, 128
Lemon Chive Beet and Boiled Egg Wrap, 45
Lemon Spinach & Egg Ribbon Soup, 105
Two-Minute Steak, Egg and Endive Salad, 82

F

Fiery Sweet Dumpling Chili, 106
fish. See also seafood.
Brazilian Fish Stew (Moqueca de Peixe), 26, 115
Bubble and Squeak Fried Potato Cakes, 142
Cajun Fish Po' Boy Wrap, 66

Grilled Eggplant RollUps, 69
Grilled Mahi Mahi "NiÇoise" Salad, 88
Portable Primal Smoked Trout Pâté, 172
Salmon and Zucchini Sliders, 26, 159
Spicy Salmon and Cucumber "Noodle" Salad, 87
Wild Tuna, Orange and Parsley Salad, 26, 95
Zucchini "Pasta" with Tomato Sauce, 166

G

Ginger and Spice Breakfast Sausages, 119
Ginger Scallion Sweet Potato Cakes, 133
goat
    Creamy Indian Goat Curry, 112
    Lamb "Dosa" Purses with Coconut Crème, 70–72
grapefruit. See Spicy Crab, Avocado and Grapefruit
    Nori Rolls.
Grilled Eggplant RollUps, 69
Grilled Mahi Mahi "NiÇoise" Salad, 88

H

ham
    Curried Green Eggs and Ham, 26, 122
    Smoked Ham and Melon Wrap with Truffle Oil,
        18, 35
Happy Valley Ranch Salad Dressing, 18, 99, 181
Hassle-Free Homemade Mayonnaise, 180
Hearts of Palm, Shrimp and Avocado Salad, 91
Herbed Omelet with Truffle Butter, 128
Homemade Mexican Chorizo Sausage, 76, 124

I

Indian-Spiced Roasted Winter Squash, 26, 171

L

lamb
    Lamb "Dosa" Purses with Coconut Crème, 70–72
    Lamb Mango Curry Wrap, 26, 73
    Lamb Sausage with Peppers and Herbs, 131
    Lamb Tzatziki Gyros in Coconut Crepes, 80
    Moroccan Meatballs, 162
    Poached Egg with Tuscan Breakfast Hash, 26, 141
lemon
    Bacon, Lemon and Greens Egg Muffins, 18, 26, 138
    Lemon Chicken and Veggie Wrap, 50
    Lemon, Chive, Beet and Boiled Egg Wrap, 45
    Lemon Pepper Roasted Chicken, 149
    Lemon Spinach & Egg Ribbon Soup, 105
    Lemony Paprika Aioli, 182
    Macadamia Lemon Pesto, 182
    Portable Primal Smoked Trout Pâté, 172
    Roast Beef and Celeriac Slaw Wrap, 49
    Salmon and Zucchini Sliders, 26, 159
    Turkey Apple Bacon Wrap with Lemon Herb
        Sauce, 44
    Winter Beet Salad with Orange and Fennel, 26, 96
    Zucchini, Prosciutto and Basil Pinwheels, 56
lobster. See seafood.

M

Macadamia Lemon Pesto, 182
mangoes. See Lamb Mango Curry Wrap.
melons
    Melon and Ginger Morning Smoothie, 145
    Smoked Ham and Melon Wrap with Truffle
        Oil, 18, 35
    Strawberry Watermelon Mint Smoothie, 146
Mexican Chorizo Tacos, 18, 76

Monterey Bay Aquarium Seafood Watch, 21
Moroccan Meatballs, 162
Moroccan Meatballs in Sweet Potato Crepes, 26, 74
mushrooms
    Chinese Ginger Pork Wrap, 77
    Creamy Indian Goat Curry, 112
    Lemon Spinach & Egg Ribbon Soup, 105
    Shrimp Coconut Lemongrass Soup, 110
    Superhero Chicken Liver Pâté, 163

N

No-Stress Homemade Chicken Stock, 103, 156
nuts and seeds
    Chicken Cranberry Salad and Fennel Wrap, 46
    Creamy Cashew Gado Gado Sauce, 18, 92, 100, 178
    Macadamia Lemon Pesto, 182
    Prosciutto and Fig Salad, 86
    Smoked Duck Wrap with Cherries and
        Hazelnuts, 40
    Vietnamese "Bun" with Pork Teriyaki, 18, 85

O

oranges
    Avocado, Orange and Herb Chicken Wrap, 39
    Butternut Parsnip Soup with Leeks, 116
    Orange Fennel Carrot Soup, 103
    Pulled Pork with Orange and Herbs, 26, 75, 148
    Wild Tuna, Orange and Parsley Salad, 26, 95
    Winter Beet Salad with Orange and Fennel, 26, 96

P

Pastrami and Pickles in Radicchio Wrap, 55
peaches. See Chicken and Peach Firecracker Wrap.
pears
    Cosmopolitan Turkey Salad and Pear Wrap, 57
    Pear, Sage and Fennel Morning Sausages, 132
peppers
    Asian Chicken "Noodle" Bowl, 92
    Brazilian Fish Stew (Moqueca de Peixe), 26, 115
    Chicken and Peach Firecracker Wrap, 28
    Cinnamon Beef in a Sweet Potato Pocket, 64
    Crisp Veggie and Turkey Rollup, 18, 38
    Fiery Sweet Dumpling Chili, 106
    Homemade Mexican Chorizo Sausage, 76, 124
    Peppery Smooth Gazpacho, 113
    Portable Tuscan Wrap, 31
    Shrimp Coconut Lemongrass Soup, 110
    Spicy Lobster Boats, 65
    Steak Salad with Curry Pickled Vegetables, 100
    Tortilla Española with Chorizo, 134
    Turkey Avocado and Spicy Pepper Wrap, 58
    Wild Tuna, Orange and Parsley Salad, 26, 95
Peppery Smooth Gazpacho, 113
pineapple
    Pineapple Bacon and Chicken Wrap, 52
    Spicy Shrimp Salad Wrap, 63
Poached Egg with Tuscan Breakfast Hash, 26, 141
pork
    Bacon and Egg Salad with Fresh Herbs, 18, 167
    Bacon and Egg Wrap with Sundried Tomato, 35
    Bacon, Lemon and Greens Egg Muffins, 18, 26, 138
    Baking Your Bacon, 153
    Bubble and Squeak Fried Potato Cakes, 142
    Cherry Tarragon Breakfast Sausages, 121
    Chicken and Peach Firecracker Wrap, 28
    Chicken Avocado Bacon Salad, 99

Chinese Ginger Pork Wrap, 77
Curried Green Eggs and Ham, 26, 122
Fiery Sweet Dumpling Chili, 106
Ginger and Spice Breakfast Sausages, 119
Homemade Mexican Chorizo Sausage, 76, 124
Lamb "Dosa" Purses with Coconut Crème, 70–72
Lamb Tzatziki Gyros in Coconut Crepes, 80
Pear, Sage and Fennel Morning Sausages, 132
Pineapple Bacon and Chicken Wrap, 52
Poached Egg with Tuscan Breakfast Hash, 26, 141
Portable Tuscan Wrap, 31
Prosciutto and Fig Salad, 86
Pulled Pork with Orange and Herbs, 26, 75, 148
Pulled Pork Wrap with Sauerkraut and
    Avocado, 26, 75
Roasted Chicken, Delicata Squash and
    Bacon Wrap, 60
Smoked Ham and Melon Wrap with Truffle
    Oil, 18, 35
Superhero Chicken Liver Pâté, 163
Sweet Apple Spice Breakfast Sausages, 18, 132
Turkey Apple Bacon Wrap with Lemon Herb
    Sauce, 44
Turkey Apricot Dijon Wrap, 34
Vietnamese "Bun" with Pork Teriyaki, 18, 85
Zucchini, Prosciutto and Basil Pinwheels, 56
Portable Primal Smoked Trout Pâté, 172
Portable Tuscan Wrap, 31
prosciutto
    Portable Tuscan Wrap, 31
    Prosciutto and Fig Salad, 86
    Zucchini, Prosciutto and Basil Pinwheels, 56
Pulled Pork with Orange and Herbs, 26, 75, 148
Pulled Pork Wrap with Sauerkraut and
    Avocado, 26, 75

R

radishes
    Asian Chicken "Noodle" Bowl, 92
    Cosmopolitan Turkey Salad and Pear Wrap, 57
    Lemon Chicken and Veggie Wrap, 50
    Spicy Crab, Avocado and Grapefruit Nori Rolls, 43
    Spicy Shrimp Salad Wrap, 63
    Steak Salad with Curry Pickled Vegetables, 100
    Vietnamese "Bun" with Pork Teriyaki, 18, 85
    Wild Tuna, Orange and Parsley Salad, 26, 95
Roast Beef and Celeriac Slaw Wrap, 49
Roast Beef and Tomato Wrap with Ginger Sauce, 53
Roasted Chicken, Delicata Squash and Bacon
    Wrap, 60
Roasted Delicata Squash, 176

S

salads
    Asian Chicken "Noodle" Bowl, 92
    Bacon and Egg Salad with Fresh Herbs, 18, 167
    Chicken Avocado Bacon Salad, 99
    Chicken, Celeriac and Mustard Salad Wrap, 32
    Chicken Cranberry Salad and Fennel Wrap, 46
    Cosmopolitan Turkey Salad and Pear Wrap, 57
    Grilled Mahi Mahi "NiÇoise" Salad, 88
    Happy Valley Ranch Salad Dressing, 18, 99, 181
    Hearts of Palm, Shrimp and Avocado Salad, 91
    Prosciutto and Fig Salad, 86
    Spicy Lobster Boats, 65
    Spicy Salmon and Cucumber "Noodle" Salad, 87
    Spicy Shrimp Salad Wrap, 63

Steak Salad with Curry Pickled Vegetables, 100
Two-Minute Steak, Egg and Endive Salad, 82
Vietnamese "Bun" with Pork Teriyaki, 18, 85
Wild Tuna, Orange and Parsley Salad, 26, 95
Winter Beet Salad with Orange and Fennel, 26, 96
salami. See Portable Tuscan Wrap.
Salmon and Zucchini Sliders, 26, 159
sauerkraut
Effortless Egg Rolls with Pickled Vegetables, 79
Pulled Pork Wrap with Sauerkraut and
     Avocado, 26, 75
Sauerkraut Made Simple, 75, 79, 183
Steak Salad with Curry Pickled Vegetables, 100
Savenor's Market, 21, 22
seafood. See also fish.
Brazilian Fish Stew (Moqueca de Peixe), 26, 115
Crabby Morning Egg Muffins, 125
Hearts of Palm, Shrimp and Avocado Salad, 91
Shrimp Coconut Lemongrass Soup, 110
Spicy Crab, Avocado and Grapefruit Nori Rolls, 43
Spicy Lobster Boats, 65
Spicy Shrimp Salad Wrap, 63
Thai Curry Crab Cakes to Go, 161
Sea-Salted Rosemary Chive Crackers, 18, 175
seeds. See nuts and seeds.
Shrimp Coconut Lemongrass Soup, 110
shrimp. See seafood.
side dishes
Bacon and Egg Salad with Fresh Herbs, 18, 167
"Cheesy" Kale Chips, 18, 168
Crunchy Root Chips, 164
Indian-Spiced Roasted Winter Squash, 26, 171
Moroccan Meatballs, 162
Portable Primal Smoked Trout Pâté, 172
Roasted Chicken, Delicata Squash and
     Bacon Wrap, 60
Salmon and Zucchini Sliders, 26, 159
Sea-Salted Rosemary Chive Crackers, 18, 175
Superhero Chicken Liver Pâté, 163
Thai Curry Crab Cakes to Go, 161
Zucchini "Pasta" with Tomato Sauce, 166
Sliced Pork Teriyaki, 18, 85
Smoked Duck Wrap with Cherries and Hazelnuts, 40
Smoked Ham and Melon Wrap with Truffle Oil, 18, 35
smoothies
Blueberry Cinnamon Coconut Smoothie, 18, 26, 146
Melon and Ginger Morning Smoothie, 145
Strawberry Watermelon Mint Smoothie, 146
soups and stews
Brazilian Fish Stew (Moqueca de Peixe), 26, 115
Butternut Parsnip Soup with Leeks, 116
Chicken, Vegetable and Avocado Soup, 18, 109
Creamy Indian Goat Curry, 112
Fiery Sweet Dumpling Chili, 106
Lemon Spinach & Egg Ribbon Soup, 105
Orange Fennel Carrot Soup, 103
Peppery Smooth Gazpacho, 113
Shrimp Coconut Lemongrass Soup, 110
Spicy Crab, Avocado and Grapefruit Nori Rolls, 43
Spicy Lobster Boats, 65
Spicy Salmon and Cucumber "Noodle" Salad, 87
Spicy Shrimp Salad Wrap, 63
spinach
Bacon, Lemon and Greens Egg Muffins, 18, 26, 138
Bubble and Squeak Fried Potato Cakes, 142
Curried Green Eggs and Ham, 26, 122
Lemon Spinach & Egg Ribbon Soup, 105

squash
Butternut Parsnip Soup with Leeks, 116
Indian-Spiced Roasted Winter Squash, 26, 171
Roasted Chicken, Delicata Squash and
     Bacon Wrap, 60
Roasted Delicata Squash, 176
Steak Salad with Curry Pickled Vegetables, 100
stews. See soups and stews.
Strawberry Watermelon Mint Smoothie, 146
Sundried Tomato Rosemary Biscuits, 18, 154
Superhero Chicken Liver Pâté, 163
Sweet Apple Spice Breakfast Sausages, 18, 132
sweet potatoes
Chinese Ginger Pork Wrap, 77
Cinnamon Beef in a Sweet Potato Pocket, 64
Ginger Scallion Sweet Potato Cakes, 133
Lamb "Dosa" Purses with Coconut Crème, 70–72
Moroccan Meatballs in Sweet Potato Crepes, 26, 74
Poached Egg with Tuscan Breakfast Hash, 26, 141
Sweet Potato Apple-Cinnamon Pancakes, 18, 127
Sweet Potato Crepes with Chives, 64, 74, 157

T
Tangy Roast Beef and Beets Wrap, 37
Terrific "Teriyaki" Jerky, 18, 151
Thai Curry Crab Cakes to Go, 161
tomatoes
Bacon and Egg Wrap with Sundried Tomato, 35
Brazilian Fish Stew (Moqueca de Peixe), 26, 115
Cajun Fish Po' Boy Wrap, 66
Chicken Avocado Bacon Salad, 99
Crabby Morning Egg Muffins, 125
Fiery Sweet Dumpling Chili, 106
Grilled Eggplant RollUps, 69
Grilled Mahi Mahi "Niçoise" Salad, 88
Hearts of Palm, Shrimp and Avocado Salad, 91
Lamb Tzatziki Gyros in Coconut Crepes, 80
Moroccan Meatballs, 162
Moroccan Meatballs in Sweet Potato Crepes, 26, 74
Peppery Smooth Gazpacho, 113
Poached Egg with Tuscan Breakfast Hash, 26, 141
Roast Beef and Tomato Wrap with Ginger
     Sauce, 53
Sundried Tomato Rosemary Biscuits, 18, 154
Zucchini "Pasta" with Tomato Sauce, 166
Tortilla Española with Chorizo, 134
turkey
Cosmopolitan Turkey Salad and Pear Wrap, 57
Crisp Veggie and Turkey Rollup, 18, 38
Moroccan Meatballs, 162
Turkey Apple Bacon Wrap with Lemon Herb
     Sauce, 44
Turkey Apricot Dijon Wrap, 34
Turkey Avocado and Spicy Pepper Wrap, 58
Two-Minute Steak, Egg and Endive Salad, 82

V
Vietnamese "Bun" with Pork Teriyaki, 18, 85

W
Wild Tuna, Orange and Parsley Salad, 26, 95
Winter Beet Salad with Orange and Fennel, 26, 96
wraps
Avocado, Orange and Herb Chicken Wrap, 39
Bacon and Egg Wrap with Sundried Tomato, 35
Cajun Fish Po' Boy Wrap, 66
Chicken and Peach Firecracker Wrap, 28

Chicken, Celeriac and Mustard Salad Wrap, 32
Chicken Cranberry Salad and Fennel Wrap, 46
Chinese Ginger Pork Wrap, 77
Cinnamon Beef in a Sweet Potato Pocket, 64
Cosmopolitan Turkey Salad and Pear Wrap, 57
Crisp Veggie and Turkey Rollup, 18, 38
Effortless Egg Rolls with Pickled Vegetables, 79
Grilled Eggplant RollUps, 69
Lamb "Dosa" Purses with Coconut Crème, 70–72
Lamb Mango Curry Wrap, 26, 73
Lamb Tzatziki Gyros in Coconut Crepes, 80
Lemon Chicken and Veggie Wrap, 50
Lemon, Chive, Beet and Boiled Egg Wrap, 45
Mexican Chorizo Tacos, 18, 76
Moroccan Meatballs in Sweet Potato Crepes, 26, 74
Pastrami and Pickles in Radicchio Wrap, 55
Pineapple Bacon and Chicken Wrap, 52
Portable Tuscan Wrap, 31
Pulled Pork Wrap with Sauerkraut and
     Avocado, 26, 75
Roast Beef and Celeriac Slaw Wrap, 49
Roast Beef and Tomato Wrap with Ginger
     Sauce, 53
Roasted Chicken, Delicata Squash and Bacon
     Wrap, 60
Smoked Duck Wrap with Cherries and
     Hazelnuts, 40
Smoked Ham and Melon Wrap with Truffle
     Oil, 18, 35
Spicy Crab, Avocado and Grapefruit Nori Rolls, 43
Spicy Lobster Boats, 65
Spicy Shrimp Salad Wrap, 63
Tangy Roast Beef and Beets Wrap, 37
Turkey Apple Bacon Wrap with Lemon Herb Sauce,
     44
Turkey Apricot Dijon Wrap, 34
Turkey Avocado and Spicy Pepper Wrap, 58
Zucchini, Prosciutto and Basil Pinwheels, 56

Z
zucchini
Asian Chicken "Noodle" Bowl, 92
Salmon and Zucchini Sliders, 26, 159
Spicy Salmon and Cucumber "Noodle" Salad, 87
Vietnamese "Bun" with Pork Teriyaki, 18, 85
Zucchini "Pasta" with Tomato Sauce, 166
Zucchini, Prosciutto and Basil Pinwheels, 56